Pam Roe, later Robinson, was unprepared for her role as the first female police officer in the City of Gloucester, a small city in Eastern Ontario. Going from a life of fun, friends and summertime frolic along the shores of the St. Lawrence to the everyday miseries of the underside of life made her toughen up quickly. And each day, as she did her job, she withstood the sideways looks, snide remarks and silent antagonism of men who feared she was a threat to them in their careers.

She endured.

This is her memoir...

The Truth behind the Badge

by
Pamela Robinson
Gloucester's First Female Police Officer

V.A.M.P. Publishing
Ottawa, Ontario

Copyright 2018 by Pamela Robinson. All rights reserved.

Robinson, Pamela, 1960, author
The truth behind the badge
by Gloucester's First Female Police Officer Pamela Robinson

Paperback: ISBN 978-1-7753899-0-3
Ebook: ISBN 978-1-7753899-1-0

Visit www.TheTruthbehindtheBadge.com for more information and internet links.
Books and Ebooks are available online at Amazon.ca and Chapters.ca

Photo of author on back cover by Ima Ortega, Ortega Photography
Photos in the text are from the Pamela Robinson collection.
Cover and interior design by Budd Publishing, Ottawa, Ontario
Editor: Sally Smith

_____

The use of any part of this publication, reproduced, stored in a retrieval system, or transmitted in any form or by any means, electronic, mechanical, photocopying, recording, or otherwise, without the prior written permission of the publisher--or, in the case of photocopying or other reprographic copying, without a licence from the Canadian Copyright Licensing Agency--is an infringement of the copyright law.

DISCLAIMER

This is my story based on true facts and worked into a memoir. Some of the names have been changed to protect the privacy of individuals. Most places, calls for service, events, and businesses are from my memories and have been written as I recall them, others have been changed slightly to protect the privacy of individuals. If there is any resemblance to real people, alive or deceased, or actual incidents, they are based on memory alone.

PRINTED IN CANADA

*This book is dedicated to my family.
Murray, you were my rock throughout this entire journey, and Amanda and Victoria, you were my teammates. I could not have done it without you.
I love you all.*

Table of Contents

Preface ix
1. First Big Step 1
2. Learning the Ropes 11
3. Ontario Police College 17
4. Last Weeks of Training 23
5. On Her Own 29
6. A Fresh Start and a Wedding 39
7. Back to the Road 45
8. Not Out of the Woods Yet 61
9. A Glimmer of Hope 69
10. Deceived 79
11. New Skills and a Wide Awakening 85
12. On the Road Again, with Attitude 95
13. A New Experience 103
14. Gearing Down and Looking Toward Retirement ...117

Preface

Pam Roe was a young woman from a small city in Eastern Ontario. She completed Gr. 13 in her hometown of Brockville and was moving on to the next stage in her life. She wanted some post secondary education but wasn't sure what she wanted to study. Her interests lay in law and acting and after many discussions with family, friends and teachers she decided acting wasn't for her, so that left law.

After more discussion she decided she wasn't mature enough for University (she liked to party and have a good time!) so she chose college. The only law choices available in college at the time were Law Enforcement, Corrections or Customs. Of the three, Pam chose Law Enforcement. She registered in a two-year program at Sir Sandford Fleming College in Peterborough and after completing her program and receiving an academic achievement award, she set about looking for a career in Law Enforcement.

She was willing to move anywhere in Canada and so sent off applications to the Ontario Provincial Police, Peel Regional, Calgary Police and last to the Gloucester Police Department. In 1983, in a precedent-setting move, the Gloucester Police Department hired her as the first female officer on their Police Service. This was the beginning of a journey with an as yet unforeseen end.

Pam's 28-year journey is based on a true story and includes her encounters along the way with the Gloucester Police

Preface

Department's ol' boys network and all that that entailed. It is her hope that this story will both caution and educate the young women of today who are considering a non-traditional career, such as policing.

— 1 —

First Big Step

I was born and raised in the small city of Brockville along the shores of the St. Lawrence River in the province of Ontario. I had a pretty good home-life — Dad was a foreman in private industry, Mom stayed at home and was always available for me and my two sisters. We lived comfortably and I was expected to be civil and polite to friends, neighbours and family. Looking back, I see my life was sheltered, my friends didn't really extend to anyone who was not really of our 'class' and I had no street-smarts (didn't really need them). Thinking about this a little more, I had a more privileged life than I realized.

So why did I choose policing as my profession, with everything that goes along with it — the violence, sad stories, deception, raw life-on-the-street backdrop? Nobody in my family, immediate or extended, had either a military or a police background. Hopefully, this memoir will explain what went into my decision-making, and draw you into my life from the time I made that ingenuous decision to the time I retired.

I chummed around with a good bunch of friends and learned through those years how important my friends were to me. They are, to this day.

The Truth behind the Badge

At five foot seven, with long blonde hair past my shoulders, a quick smile and bright blue eyes, I was pretty and fun to be with. I was happy, I was positive, and I attracted people. We always had something to do and somewhere to go, a friend's cottage for the weekend or off to our old stomping ground, A-Bay (Alexandria Bay), in up-state New York. I loved to sew, I loved crafts and playing cards. We moved in a close-knit bunch of 10 girls and 10 guys who went everywhere together. We spent a lot of time on the water, water-skiing, boating or sunbathing.

I really liked the good things in life and I remember my Dad saying I'd eventually have to have a good paying job to enjoy everything I liked and wanted. As a teen I did as much as I needed in school and graduated from Gr. 13 with a 74 per cent average — not really good, not really bad.

When the time came to make a decision about what to do with my life, there were two things that appealed, acting or law. It wasn't easy deciding but with friends and family chiming in with a reality check, and after long, heated discussions, I chose law. Sometimes I think I let myself be led away from acting because, there, I could really express myself and BE myself, but the reality of an acting career was pretty dismal.

I chose college over university, and went on to post-secondary schooling in Peterborough studying Law and Security at Sir Sandford Fleming, also known as Fleming College. From that course I chose policing as my future profession.

I grew up a lot at college; I didn't just get by, as I had in high school. I got the highest grade point average for women and won an academic award for my work. Obviously I wasn't just another pretty face.

I graduated at the age of 22. There I was with a newly-minted diploma in my back pocket, a chosen path in sight and nowhere to use it.

First Big Step

I moved back in with Mom and Dad for a while but after eight months with still no job in sight, I made another decision, this one to move to Ottawa.

I moved after Christmas on a cold January day to a friend's basement apartment in a townhouse; within two weeks I had a job in security at Ottawa International Airport. This boosted my morale, and with the prospect of policing still in the back of my mind, I took some steps in that direction.

One morning, in late January, I took my resumé and headed to the nearby bus stop; I had a half-hour wait ahead of me. I was a little anxious because I was headed to the Gloucester Police Department to write exams at 9 a.m. for a constable's position, the first step in the hiring process, and I didn't want to be late.

The snow kept coming down, and coming down, and I was getting wetter and wetter. It soaked into my hair and coat, I was drenched, and still no bus. So I made a quick decision to go back home and change. I really wanted to be presentable for my interview; how I looked was important.

Before I left home the second time I called the bus station. I had 15 minutes before the bus arrived, and finally got to the Police Station with 10 minutes to spare.

But, really, all was not well when I arrived. A big, gruff white haired guy in uniform met me. I gave him my name, told him I was there to see the recruiting officer, and that I was supposed to write an exam at 9. I was getting really anxious.

Finally I was taken to a back room and asked to do a typing test; I gave myself a mental shrug, did it (remembering back to when I'd taken typing in high school), and wondered how much typing I'd have to do as a police constable. When a third person came to talk to me and started to tell me the duties of a clerk in the records department, my anxiety was replaced by the beginnings of anger. I looked him straight in the eye and firmly told him I was there to write my exams to become a police officer.

That really got his attention! He blurted out "We don't have police women here!"

"I know," I said bluntly. "I'll be the first one." That flustered him even more. I'd like to think he ran from the room, but it was probably just a quick walk. He came back quickly, too, told me to wait, once again, in the front lobby.

And there I sat. It was 1030. I'd been there an hour-and-a-half, talked to three different people, told them several times I was there to write the entrance exam, taken a useless typing test (which I'd passed with flying colours), and now was sitting, waiting, once again. Seven a.m. seemed a long time ago....

So when Sgt. Scheffer eventually walked through the front door, I was in quite a mood. He was a tall, heavy-set man, maybe intimidating to some, but I'd planned and worked for this, so I wasn't giving up now. I stood as he approached.

"I'm busy," he said abruptly. "Book an appointment if you want to see me." I was more than angry at this point. I was furious.

"I booked an appointment with you three weeks ago. My appointment was for 9 a.m. this morning. I was at the front desk at 0850, told the officer my name, who I was to see and the reason I was here. It was the ineptness of your people who put me through the test for a clerk and now you're telling me that you can't see me? They also made it very clear that you don't hire police women."

I was really steaming now, so I just carried on. I rhymed off my qualifications, shoved my resumé into his hands, and turned and walked out the door.

But that's as far as my anger took me. My throat tightened, tears filled the corners of my eyes making me stumble a bit, and I started to cry. Looking back, this should have given me a hint of what was to come.

I thought for a long time that night about what to do, and talked it over with Delia, my roommate, finally deciding to call the Chief of Police. I was surprised to get him on the line so easily, so when he answered, instead of giving him my name, I just blurted out the question — "Is Gloucester Police Force hiring?"

"Yes," he said. "But we have a lot of applications on file at the moment."

"Do you hire women?" I asked.

He got the gist, then, and asked me a question. "Is this Pam Roe by any chance?"

I was a bit taken aback, thinking I had been clever in not giving him my name.

"Yes."

I told him my side of the story — about waiting, and the typing test, and waiting some more, and then the rudeness of Sgt. Scheffer, and finally not even being able to write the entrance exams. He listened quietly and said he'd get back to me in a couple of days.

He stuck to his word. He called two days later and asked me to come back to the Station in a week to write the entrance exams. I was elated. Finally things were moving ahead. The decision to call had been a good one.

Over the next six months while going through the process to get into the police force, I had a lot of time to think. I was tested and interviewed, wrote exams and did some psychological evaluations. A background check was done, I passed physical fitness work-ups, and finally was interviewed, not once but twice — once before a board of three high ranking officers and the second time before the Police Services Board. And even while all this was happening — running on the treadmill, getting my blood pressure taken, filling in the blanks on IQs and psychological tests — my mind was racing ahead thinking if I ever had this to do again for another job I'd get it in a flash because of everything I'd had to endure so far.

My mother received the phone call saying I'd been hired. She called me at a friend's cottage. I was to start work July 4, 1983. I didn't know, then, how explosive that short call would be, but the press was on it. It was hot news — First Female Constable with Gloucester Police Department. My friends and I had a great time that night wondering what my new job would be, thinking about an actual career with the police, what it would be like, what I would be like in this new role.

So the next day at the cottage, after a long boisterous night, it was disruptive to get a call from James Brown with CTV News.

"Can I arrange an interview with you about your new police career," he asked. Startled, and a bit unsure how to react, I was prim, and, what I hope was professional, with my reply. "I start my new job on Monday, and you can interview me then," I said, and hung up.

Monday arrived. I showed up for work at 0800 hours. There were two others starting their first day, too, Norm Bisson and Justin McDougal. We'd all go to Police College in Aylmer in September but first we headed out for our swearing-in ceremony at the Court House where we promised to serve and protect our community.

That's when I really got a glimpse of what my immediate future held — the press was everywhere. I must have looked

First Big Step

like a deer caught in the headlights when I realized they were there for me. I wondered out loud what I could and couldn't say, was told to be circumspect and always professional, and left to my own quick thinking.

So the questions began.

"How does it feel to be the first police woman in Gloucester?"

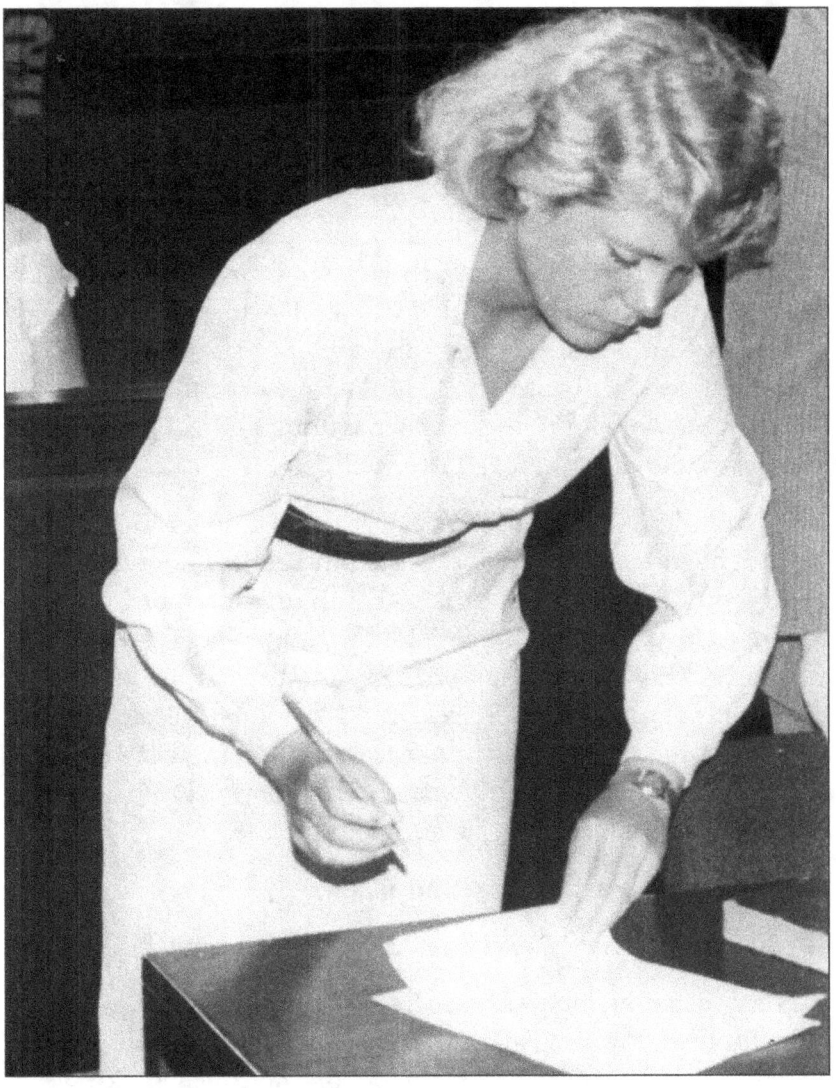

Swearing-in ceremony where we promised to serve and protect our community.

"Do you feel like a pioneer?"

"What are your favourite things to do?"

"What are your career plans?"

"Where were you born?"

"How old are you?"

I took a deep breath and answered the questions one by one. I remember giving only a fleeting thought to Bisson and McDougal (it was their first day, too), but everything was happening too fast for much more than that.

From the media scrum and swearing-in, we went back to the Station for lunch and then to the Quartermaster for uniforms. It was that day, on the way to lunch, that I got a glimpse of what my life would hold as the first female police officer in Gloucester. We met, and were introduced, to a fellow officer on the stairs. He looked me up and down, brushed past me and on the way past muttered "I guess you'll be a Sergeant before I ever will."

I was nonplussed. This was my first day, I'd never met him before, he knew nothing about me but seemed aggressively belligerent. I didn't have time to think further about this because the press weren't finished with me yet. They were waiting at the Quartermaster to get pictures of me being outfitted for a uniform. Bisson and McDougal were once again ignored while I was photographed getting fitted for my hat. And, after that when I was looking forward to heading home, I was told the Chief wanted to see me.

"How did your first day go?" he asked.

"It went well," I said, "exciting, a little unexpected."

He told me some lockers were being built into the janitor's cubbyhole and were available for my use. As I was the first female officer in Gloucester, the department was making accommodations, and he cautioned me there were to be no complaints in the meantime.

After the snide comment on the stairwell, this gave me a feeling of being included and having a place of my own, so I didn't mind much that the lockers were in a janitor's cupboard. What I really liked was being able to change into my uniform at work, not at home.

Seeing myself on the 6 o'clock news that night was a bit surreal. I went to bed reflecting on the eventful day.

—2—

Learning the Ropes

We three newbies settled into our new jobs, each with a coach officer who taught us the ropes. The officers were there with us for three months teaching us everything from how to write traffic tickets to how to investigate a murder. The end of that time was coming up fast and we'd be out on our own then, if we were ready. The hardest part throughout the months was adjusting to shift work. Not only did we have to learn everything in a short period of time, but we had to do it while adjusting to three different shifts.

Barnard Partiage was my coach. He was a Constable, 18 years on the force, had lots of freckles, liked to joke around and talked with a bit of a twang.

He swaggered when he walked, and lived in an intergenerational house — mom, dad, wife, young son and daughter. People called him Barnie.

During one afternoon shift, Barnie asked me to come home with him and meet his family. Within moments I was invited for dinner. Barnie's Mom, a great cook, did the cooking and afterwards all the adults around the table lit up cigarettes. Oh!, I thought, a little uncomfortable, but intrigued, too. My family didn't smoke, so we never sat around smoking after dinner. The after-dinner moment didn't last long, though. Barnie was on a roll, and after a few quick drags, he butted out, looked at me, said "Come on," and we were out the back door into the cruiser.

Just then the dispatcher called. "XJN385 to 3602." 3602 was our number. XJN385 was the dispatcher's.

"Go ahead," said Barnie.

"There's a 10-55 at 9721 Farmers Way."

"10-4," Barnie answered.

The dispatcher described the situation. "There's a baseball bat and chairs being thrown around." This was it, I thought. My first incident. My heart started thumping. I took a few deep breaths.

Barnie, on the other hand, was making this into a routine training session; "What's a 10-55," he asked.

I was good at this, I knew, and answered "A domestic."

Barnie grinned.

"What are we going to do when we get there?"

"Approach with caution," I said. "One take the back and one the front."

"Right," said Barnie. "Caution, for sure, but stay together. Don't get out of one another's sight. We don't have another person, so no one's taking the back."

That slipped by me for a moment. My mind was rapidly running through "Is someone going to be hurt? Are we going to end up in a fight? What does the house look like? What do the people look like? What will happen once we arrive? What actually happened?"

I abruptly came back to what he said. "Why do we always keep one another in sight?" I asked.

"Because all people react differently to police. If we end up arresting someone, other family members might get belligerent. Once I went to a domestic and the wife suddenly jumped on my partner's back and started pounding him.

"The people involved are irrational. They call because they want help, but if you make a step towards arresting someone they love, they lose it, they're furious, want to take it out on you."

Uh-oh. I could feel my anxiety level skyrocketing.

This was a crunch for me, travelling at top speed, lights and siren on, listening to what's happening in the car and on the radio at the same time. But while all this was zooming through my head, dispatch sent a second unit for backup.

Barnie pulled into the long driveway. Lights were blazing inside the bungalow. Outside, dilapidated cars, trucks and farm machinery littered the front lawn.

"Follow my lead," he yelled, jumping out of the car. He turned back quickly gesturing to me to be quiet. "Listen," he mouthed.

I easily picked up what was happening inside.

"What the fuck do you think you're doing?" a man hollered. I heard furniture smashing and a woman pleading "Don't hurt me, just don't hurt me."

Barnie stormed to the door. He knocked. No answer. He knocked again. "Gloucester Police, open up!"

A teenage boy pulled it open. "My Mom and Dad. They're in the kitchen." He was scared. When I went in I saw why. An upturned chair lay askew in the middle of the table among beer bottles; carving knives were scattered across the counter. A man sat, a woman stood across from him in a doorway, panting, arms covered in bruises.

As Barnie moved forward, a third officer barged through the door into the kitchen. The man started cursing, spitting out the story. The teenager, emboldened by the presence of police, yelled, too.

"Yeah…and what about the chair you threw? Did you see the size of the bruise Mom has? Look. Here's the bat he threatened her with."

It was obvious to all of us the guy was drunk. Barnie signalled me to take the woman into another room while he and the other officer spoke to the father.

This was her story. Her husband arrived home and started to drink. She was making dinner but didn't make it fast enough or to his liking; he started to argue. When she'd heard enough, she threw down the spatula, told him to make his own dinner and started to leave the kitchen. Her husband picked up a baseball bat and threatened her. "If you don't get back here and make my dinner the way I want it, you won't live any longer." She went back and carried on cooking.

As she cooked, her husband continued to berate and criticize her, and continued drinking. When dinner was ready, she placed it in front of him and left. He yelled at her to get back and eat with him. She refused. He picked up a chair and threw it at her. She turned, saw the chair coming and blocked it with her arm. It bounced off onto the table.

After he'd finished with the guy, Barnie listened to my version, agreed both the wife and teen's were the same, and said he was going to arrest the man for assault. He asked me to get a written statement from the boy and his mother, and to take the baseball bat and chair for evidence. Then he left.

It took an hour-and-a-half for Barnie to get back to the house. During that time I took statements, tagged the chair and bat, and waited.

It wasn't much fun from that point on; it took three hours to prepare a court brief, and the Sergeant had to approve it before we could submit it. Even then we weren't through; we had to lodge the property in the property room. Finally Barnie said goodbye, I'll see you tomorrow.

It was a steep learning curve and every day brought something different. Afternoon shifts went from 1600 to 2400 hours and I always arrived early to prepare and get ready for line-up. During line-up we were briefed on what could happen, from prisoners being released to which officers were assigned to which duties. Then we hit the road.

That day we took a minor call — barking dog — but mostly wrote tickets. Barnie showed me how to run radar and write a Provincial Offence Notice. Most of the time we patrolled the area.

Barnie told me I had to become familiar with my area in order to notice if things were out of place.

"What do you mean, out of place?"

"Well, take for example, the shops in your area. If you know what time they open and close, you'll know who, if anyone, should be around during the off hours. You'll also notice if the windows are broken. Midnight shift is when you'll see most of these things."

I soaked all this in like a sponge. The rest of the shift was quiet which gave me time to think about what Barnie'd said. I was going to be on my own pretty soon, so I had to remember.

A couple of weeks later on midnight shift we found a vehicle sitting at the side of the road with its headlights on but not running; no one was in or near it. I ran the licence plate and it came back 'not stolen.' Just then we saw a lanky figure carrying a jerry can walking towards us. He stopped, asked if there was a problem, and when we said there wasn't, he explained he'd run out of gas and walked to get more.

That seemed to be the end of it but about an hour later an officer radioed he was following a vehicle that was acting suspiciously. He said the driver was driving the back streets deliberately trying to avoid the police cruiser; when he described the car it fit the one Barnie and I'd seen earlier. So we whipped around and headed off to corner him.

As soon as the driver saw our lights he drove over the curb and up a steep hill. Barnie followed, the curb dragged at the undercarriage, and the other car got a good lead. He stopped at the top, bailed out and ran. We lost him.

It was then dispatch told us the car was stolen, so Barnie and I were now dealing with a stolen vehicle.

We were really frustrated. Only an hour earlier we'd seen the guy, talked to him, and now he was gone. Barnie, a little more philosophical and with many more years under his belt than me, said, "Well...we didn't get him this time, but always remember, time is on our side." That stuck with me the rest of my career.

—3—

Ontario Police College

September 1983 rolled around in the blink of an eye. The three of us left for our initial training at The Ontario Police College. This was part one (nine weeks) of legislated training that all new police recruits in Ontario go through, with part two (six weeks) following shortly after.

Ontario Police College (OPC) is located in rural countryside near small-town Aylmer, Ontario. Mennonite communities surround the College and two larger cities, St.Thomas and London, are within an hour's drive. In 1963 OPC offered its first classes at an abandoned Royal Canadian Air Force Base. In 1976 the College opened its doors at its current site.

I took my own car and Norm Bisson took his; it was a six hour drive from Ottawa and we made it in good time. Once there we checked in at the front desk and found our rooms. The men's facilities were separate from the women's and the rooms were organized into pods.

Each pod had an upper and lower level with one toilet, one shower, and two sinks on each level. There were four rooms on the bottom and four on the top with one person to each room. The rooms had sealed windows, brown brick walls, a single bed, and a built-in desk with a shelf above. The floor was covered with rust coloured, indoor/outdoor carpeting. There was a small, walk-in closet with a mirror in each room and each pod had a common area. This area was used for group studying and gatherings. I unpacked and set up my room the way I wanted. I like having familiar things around me so I'd brought a pillow, a comfy duvet and some comfortable clothes.

I had mixed feelings at check in. I was excited, nervous, anxious because I didn't know anyone else except the two guys from back home. I didn't know what the college grounds were like, so as no one else had checked in, I walked around by myself. I found the cafeteria, pool and work-out facilities, along with the gym, the bar, the library and finally the classrooms. I eventually headed back to my room and settled in for the evening. Breakfast was at 0800 hours, classes started at 0900 hours; I set my alarm for 0700 hours in order to get everything done I wanted to beforehand.

Next morning, set for the day, I headed to the cafeteria to find out what the college offered in the way of food. There was everything from bacon and eggs, to cereal. Not being a real breakfast-eater, I stuck to toast and coffee and carried them to a seat at one of the long tables. There were a few others in the cafeteria, some in groups, others by themselves.

After breakfast, I headed to the classroom. I was early but soon others trickled in and found seats. There were officers from Peel Region, Toronto, Ottawa, the OPP, Barrie, Waterloo Regional, Sarnia, Brockville and London. When 0900 hours clicked in, class began. We introduced ourselves and learned the teacher was seconded from Waterloo Regional. We all received timetables and it was only now I learned what classes I'd take — Provincial Statutes, Criminal Code, Physical Education, Practical Scenarios, Drill, Powers of Arrest, Search and Seizure, Court Proceedings, Evidence, Pistol and Handcuffing Techniques.

After lunch was phys ed so I didn't eat much; I knew we had to run one-and-a-half miles each phys ed session with no exceptions. The runs were timed and each person had to reach a particular time for their age and gender in order to pass the final exam. I wanted to pass first try; that would give me one less thing to worry about. After the run we could go to the pool or the weight room.

After phys ed we showered, cleaned up and went to class. Classes ended at 1600 hours and we were free to do what we wanted. We were encouraged to participate in extracurricular activities to fill up the time. Dinner was served at 1700 hours.

After dinner there was free time unless you were on Station Duty. Each student had to do Station Duty at least twice during the two semesters. This meant securing inner and outer perimeters of the College by walking them, and making sure the grounds were safe. Any breaches had to be reported in the duty book with names and details. Students wore full uniform, including forage cap and red arm band; duty lasted from 2300 to 0100 hours, and class started at 0900 hours the next morning. That meant a really long day but we all had to do it.

After a few weeks I'd met everyone in my pod and classes. Any spare time I had was spent on my boots and homework. Each day every recruit had to pass uniform inspection and once a week room inspection. If you didn't pass, your Chief was notified. And, if you didn't pass academically, your career could be jeopardized.

Rather than face the long drive back to Ottawa on weekends, we three decided to stay at the College. Very few stayed, and this meant the cafeteria was closed down Saturdays and Sundays. The campus became like a ghost town — quiet, boring, nothing to look forward to. Five weeks into training, I hated it, hated it! I was lonely, I was bored, there was nothing to do outside of College, and with only 20 other females around out of 550 students, we were pretty much a group unto ourselves. We supported each other in our endeavours, but we didn't chum around much.

When I was away at Sir Sandford Fleming, I had lots of friends. My marks were good and the group I hung around with was similar to my home group. But here? I wasn't making many female friends, especially with the women from Peel. They were really competitive, very elitist. Just to get accepted at Peel their marks had to be high, and they made sure to tell us how high they had to be. According to them, they were much higher than all the other departments. So we weren't a close-knit group.

The guys were worse. Sometimes I'd go to the bar with my friend Fergie (Ross Ferguson) from the Brockville Police Service. Right off the bat we'd hit it off because we had something in common — Brockville. I liked him. He was like the guys back home, both respectful and teasing. He loved his wife (they were just newly married), and I felt comfortable and safe with him. He was a good friend and I needed a friend then.

But if Fergie wasn't at the bar, I was hit on by drunks, or even married men. It was obvious they were married because not only did they keep their rings on while trying to pick me up but often the conversation centred around their eight-month pregnant wives back home!

I think some of the women who'd been hired honestly felt they had to be really tough, had to become one of the guys to make it; others felt they had to sleep their way to the top. But that wasn't me. To me, the whole idea of sleeping around was distasteful and immoral — not that I was a snob or a prig — but because I had a very clear vision of what I thought police officers were like, and my upbringing had taught me to have respect, and show respect. The reality of College life nearly

Initial Training at Ontario Police College

drummed that out of me. I made a vow at that time never to date a cop, let alone marry one.

Boy...was I wrong!

Ever so slowly the weeks passed. I was counting down...then there were three weeks to go, 21 days. I'd only been home twice and found when I had to leave to go back to College, I was feeling sad and low even though I knew the time was almost up. The time at College had really been long, lonely and tedious. I missed the ease and familiarity of my normal routine and life.

I'd known from the beginning of training that I'd have to pass my run within a certain time and so I'd been running extra miles in off hours with a running partner, Wayne Rosko from Metro Toronto Police. Wayne was the best runner in the class. Not only that, he was fit, good looking and loved to laugh. When he ran, I watched. He ran effortlessly, with grace and elegance. I ran with him twice a week and saw a big improvement in my time and endurance. And at the end, I did it. I ran one-and-a-half miles in 10 minutes 24 seconds, passing with flying colours. Wayne was at the finish line cheering me on.

Final exams came and went. I passed everything and after packing, with barely a second thought, jumped in the car and headed home with only a small niggle in the back of my head...I had to return to the College in four months for the second semester.

— 4 —

Last Weeks of Training

On my second dayshift back from college I was assigned to prisoner escort duty with Edward Svlofski. We had to take two prisoners from the cell block to the courthouse for show-cause hearings. Svlofski was one of those guys who looked, dressed and worked by the book. He showed respect, was kind, his uniform was pressed just so, and his boots glistened.

We met at the cell block, took the prisoners out of the cell, handcuffed them and shackled them at the ankles. Svlofski searched them before we headed out making sure there was nothing they could use to harm themselves or us. One was a 23-year-old Rastafarian labelled as a 'rounder' in the system. He knew what to expect. The 17-year-old, on the other hand, was new to the system and didn't have a clue. Both wore jeans, T-shirts and running shoes.

We got to the courthouse at 0850 hours, Svlofski checked their handcuffs again noting it in his book, and we opened the back doors. In a flash, they were gone. It happened so fast I stood stock still for a moment and then the adrenaline kicked in. Svlofski ran after one and I ran like hell after the other, thinking as I was pounding along the pavement through rush hour traffic that this was just like the movies.

All that running training surfaced. I ran up over the trunk of a car stopped in traffic, over a break wall, fence and down a sidewalk. But I was wearing 25 pounds of equipment and gear while he had only a T-shirt, sneakers and jeans on; I was beginning to breathe hard.

I started yelling. "Stop that guy!" Two men in morning traffic jumped out of their cars and grabbed the runner. I was only seconds behind. I thanked them, a little out-of-breath, looked the runner straight in the eye and told him to smarten up.

"Don't try that again! You can add escape lawful custody to your list of charges," I ranted at him as we headed back to the courthouse. Svlofski caught his runner, too, but because of the attempted escape both of us had to write an occurrence report. We learned later that the Rastafarian had a paper clip in his braids which he bent into a pin and used to undo the shackles.

I was still on an adrenalin high when we got back to the station and immediately started telling Barnie about the escapees that morning. Putting on his teacher's hat, he took a more cautionary approach. "Don't talk to others about this. It has to be investigated," he said. This settled me down with a crash. Had we done something wrong? I didn't think so but this was the first time anything I'd done had to be investigated by the powers-that-be. Barnie assured me this was pretty routine and the purpose was to exonerate officers. He was right, and I was a worry-wart, because three weeks later we were cleared. I did take to heart Barnie's caution about following procedure in all situations, though.

The weeks went on. On a midnight shift, with Barnie in the car, I spotted a car making swooping weaves from the centre-line to the gravel shoulder and back again. Barnie told me to catch up and pace it.

This was another teaching moment. I listened as Barnie outlined what I should observe and do — watch whether the road was straight and level, whether there was a curve or hill, note the distance I followed the vehicle and the speed I was travelling. When I stopped him I'd have to make some quick observations — glassy-eyed, slurred speech, odour of alcohol, lack of coordination. And Barnie told me to pull him over in a well-lit area.

With all that running through my mind, he gave me the thumbs up and said, "You're on your own." He was going to watch.

I put my lights on. When the car ahead stopped, I walked to the driver's door.

"Do you know why I'm stopping you?" I asked.

"No."

Coming from the open window I could smell alcohol. I asked him for his driver's licence, registration and insurance. He fumbled with his wallet, dropped his insurance, and after a search found his registration. As we walked back to the cruiser, Barnie asked what I was going to do.

"I'm going to arrest him for impaired driving."

I went through all the reasons why. Barnie agreed and called a second unit to tow the vehicle. I went back to the driver. He was pretty unsteady when he got out of the car. I cuffed him, Barnie searched him. I read him his rights and told him why he was under arrest.

I kept good notes, and back at the station asked for a breath technician; eventually I learned he blew 2.70 and 2.40. Those were high readings considering the legal limit was .80 mgs/100 mls. blood. I put him in a cell to sober up. He was released the next morning.

Next came the paper work. Barnie, a bit amused, told me I'd need "one of those, one of those, one of those, one of those, and one of those." I knew I was in for a long haul. It took me two hours to finish.

Even though I knew it was coming, I was not really ready when Barnie told me at the end of our shift that he wouldn't be there on our first dayshift. I was going to ride with another officer or maybe on my own. Before any of that could really settle in, we said our goodbyes for the weekend and I went home.

My roommate, Laura Delaney, and I had planned a housewarming party and while my mind was partly on that, rolling around in the back of my head was the possibility that I'd be on my own come Monday. When I had some quiet time and started thinking about it, my nerves kicked in. The reasoning part of my brain, though, said, a little sternly (like my Dad might say) "You gotta jump sometime," and I knew I could always call Barnie if I had a question. I wasn't fully confident, but I was ready.

I slept in Saturday morning, and the rest of the day prepared for the party. We'd invited 20 people; they were coming for 1900 hours. Everybody was there and the party was in full swing when the phone rang at 2200 hours. It was for me, work calling. They wanted me to do a search on a female arrested for drugs. This wasn't the first time I'd been asked, and I didn't mind, except tonight I'd been drinking. So I told the dispatcher "No" and she said they'd find someone else. I knew that before I'd been hired some of the women in the office had done the searches. I felt sure the task was covered.

Back at it Monday morning I worked dispatch and when the afternoon shift came in I was to go on the road with Constable Nic Soloman. On dispatch I worked with Constable Gus Leudroil. Leudroil was nice, easy to talk to and I felt comfortable around him. He was a good teacher, patient and efficient when it came to dispatch.

As the morning wore on we got to know one another. At one point Sergeant Joel Scissons walked by and said something to Leudroil. I didn't catch what he said but heard Leudroil say, "You better. She didn't deserve that."

Leudroil caught my eye and explained the gist of the comment.

"Did you have a party Saturday night?"

"Yes."

"Did you get a phone call from work?"

"Yes."

"It was Scissons who wanted you called to do the search and when you couldn't come in he broadcast over the air, "Well, if a party is more important than her career, I guess we'll have to get someone else."

The guys gave him a hard time about that and told him you had every right to have a party and he owed you an apology."

I was surprised. Just then Scissons walked by again and stopped. He looked directly at me and said he was sorry.

"I shouldn't have said what I said over the air."

I was a bit disconcerted, but always polite, I smiled and said, "No need to apologize. It was a good party." Scissons smiled, accepting my unstated offer of a truce, and left. Again, in my naiveté, I didn't give it too much thought.

It was lunch time and Leudroil told me to take a break. "By the time you're done, Soloman should be in on afternoons and you can go out on the road."

An hour later Soloman showed up, introduced himself and said he'd wait for me at the south doors with a cruiser.

We patrolled around the south end for about an hour, all the time talking and getting to know each other. He used to work for the Calgary Police and had only been in Gloucester two years although he was originally from Ottawa.

"I had a problem in Calgary," he admitted, "...with a female officer."

I turned in the seat to look at him, briefly catching his eye as he was driving.

"Well you won't have a problem with this female because she's not the same one," I said quietly and assertively. It's only in hindsight that I realize now it was at that moment I cracked open Pandora's box — the worry, the hate, the envy, the bullying and maliciousness.

Next day I was back working with Barnie. He said I was ready to venture out on my own at the end of my day shift weeks. That meant 12 more shifts with a partner and then on my own. Barnie assured me that even though I was "on my own" I really wasn't, as I could always ask for help. That was comforting. I was sure I'd come across situations and not have a clue what to do next, so his words were really understanding.

The final shift ended. Barnie handed me the performance review he'd written, complimentary of my work, and as I walked away after a smile and a hug, I felt I'd made a good start.

—5—

On Her Own

Each new officer, once trained, is assigned to a platoon. I was assigned to "A" Platoon and followed their schedule. Nic Soloman was on my platoon as well, and our Sergeant was Sergeant Gerald.

I wanted to do the best I could, both for me and Barnie, who had been such a good mentor. I always tried to arrive about a half hour before my shift began, so on my first shift I arrived early, picked up the keys to the cruiser, and did my vehicle equipment check before briefing. Once out there, I really wanted to learn my zone inside out. I knew the city was divided into eight zones, four upper and four lower. I was assigned to zone 104, an upper zone; the lower ones were the busiest in the city.

After a couple of hours, dispatch came over the radio and called out units 101, 102 and 103, not mine. No one responded, so when the dispatcher called the Sergeant explaining no one had responded to an accident call, the Sergeant told him to call me. I couldn't figure this out for awhile. The accident was in my zone but I wasn't called. Then it hit me, and I started laughing. They didn't have any police women before, and now that they did, they didn't know what to do with me. That bit of intuitive insight kept me going all day.

Three weeks in and things were going smoothly. One midnight shift Gerald told me I'd be guarding Michelle Jollie in the cell block; she'd been arrested for murder. It was a pretty gruesome story. Michelle lived with her boyfriend and nine-month-old son on the fifth floor of an apartment building. But Michelle had found a new guy on the third floor and persuaded him to beat up the old one. Her plan was to drop a key over the side of the balcony to the new guy and go back to bed. He'd let himself in, beat up the father of her son, and leave.

The new guy had other plans; he stabbed the old boyfriend 43 times.

Detective Boisvert was investigating the case. He was going to lay charges in the morning. As we walked towards the cell he told me I'd have to caution Michelle again and explain to her that I'd be there guarding her throughout the night; if she wanted anything, like a blanket or a cup of tea, I'd be there to get it. Boisvert introduced us and I cautioned Michelle telling her if she said anything in relation to the murder I'd write it down and it could be used against her in court. She nodded her head. She understood.

This was a new experience for me. I figured it would be a long night so I pulled my chair from the hallway to sit directly outside her cell where we could talk.

Michelle asked a good question right off the bat, like why did I become a police officer. I really didn't want her to know, actually thinking it was none of her business, so answered by asking her a question.

Over the hours Michelle talked more and more about all kinds of things — making jam, her baby boy, gardening. Suddenly she blurted "It wasn't supposed to be that way, it wasn't supposed to happen."

"What wasn't supposed to be what way? What wasn't supposed to happen?" I asked, immediately aware the whole tone of the conversation had changed.

Michelle confessed everything. She told me how her new boyfriend killed the old one, how she had dropped the key down to him so he could unlock the door to the apartment.

I didn't re-caution her, I just started taking notes.

"Don't pay any attention to me, just tell me whatever comes to mind," I said. The night wasn't so long after all. I wrote, and wrote and wrote some more. By the end of the night I had about 50 pages.

Michelle eventually trailed off and fell asleep around 0300 hours. Not me. I went over my notes to make sure I understood my scribbling so when I reported in I'd have everything straight.

First thing next morning Boisvert called me to his office and asked how things went.

"Michelle told me everything," I said. Boisvert was more than delighted. "F-u-u-u-ck," he said. "She gave you a full confession. Get me two copies of your notes before you leave this morning."

He actually patted me on the back, which I accepted as a job well done, and told me I'd see him in court. I was elated; if this was what my job was going to be like in the future it was going to be pretty darn good.

I left for home to get some sleep.

Looking back now, I see that praise for me made Soloman seethe. I was high on approval, the job I was doing, the sense of achievement I was feeling; he was writhing with envy, black with anger. If I'd known, I'd have recognized it as a dark omen, a warning in the wind. He was more than uncomfortable with my success. I was a threat to him and he set out to make my life miserable.

Months passed. I was doing well, making arrests, conducting traffic stops and testifying in court. I'd received commendations from Crown attorneys, defence lawyers and members of the public. I went to social events with the Chief of Police because I was Gloucester's 'token' female. I was in the spotlight...and Wow! Did it feel fake to me! I stood there beside the Chief, no mingling, smile pasted on my face, just a show piece. My 'inside' voice said it was them saying, "Look. We hire women." There wasn't much I could do about it then. Today, I would react differently.

Chief Thompson and the "token female" at a community event

Eventually I requested a transfer to the lower end, the busy end, and I got it. My thinking was, because it was busier, there would be more content and I'd be learning new skills. My zone was 212, the Beacon Hill area of Gloucester.

On Her Own

During this time, enjoying the limelight and the busy work schedule, I met an officer by the name of Murray Robinson… and fell in love.

He was a good looking guy with a beautiful smile, blue eyes and thick brown hair. As far as I knew he was a gentleman but, even so, when he showed up alongside my cruiser one day and asked me out, I said no. I didn't want to mix business with pleasure.

How quickly I regretted that decision! Murray had all the qualities I was looking for in a partner, so I took a chance a couple of days later, flirted a bit, and said, "If the invitation's still open, I'd like to take you up on it."

He grinned. "Are you going to Norm's BBQ this weekend"?

I nodded.

"I'll see you there and we can discuss dinner plans."

A whirlwind wooing followed. We were inseparable. We did everything together. But it was the closeness and togetherness that, at times, pricked my conscience. I didn't know how the Chief or my colleagues would see this and I sure didn't want to put our careers in jeopardy.

I decided I had to go to the Chief and get his approval before continuing along this path. I talked to Murray. "If the Chief doesn't agree, we'll have to break up." I was pretty adamant about this; I'd worked hard to get here and wasn't willing to give it up for someone I'd just met.

Murray was reluctant, but he agreed even though he knew if the Chief was wary about the situation, or hesitated even a bit when I asked him, that I would break up with him.

The Chief was very cool and considered. I explained it wasn't a problem yet, but could be down the road.

"Your work day is your work day. Your own time is your personal time. As far as I'm concerned as long as your personal time doesn't interfere with your work, whatever you want to do is your business."

Murray was thrilled. So was I.

The next step was dealing with our colleagues. We planned to introduce ourselves as a couple slowly. I spent a lot of time at Murray's place in the village of Osgoode and two other Gloucester police officers lived on the same street. They saw us together all the time and so we told them first; we started to be seen at social functions and everyone quickly became aware that we were a couple. There were times, though, I'd get glares from other police officers' wives. I wrote this off as my own insecurity, not theirs, but realized over time it was really their insecurity, not mine. I didn't go after their husbands, it wasn't my style. So their opinion soon mattered less and less.

It was about now that little things started surfacing with Soloman. I realized he was excluding me, leaving me out of the team. Even when I backed him on calls, when it was over he'd high five the others, but never me; it was as if I wasn't there. And he began to complain to Gerald about my work. On one particular call, Soloman had been dispatched about a suspicious person in the neighbourhood. I was the last to arrive on scene. The rest of them had their lights off waiting to see if this person would walk out into the street. When I arrived, with my lights on, and drove up to get an up-date, Soloman told me really forcefully they were about to clear from the call and next time I came to a call like this I'd better have my headlights off. His delivery was short and nasty.

The next day he took his complaint directly to Gerald. Gerald called me into his office and dressed me down taking Soloman at his word. He told me I'd better start approaching work differently because, if not, it would be reflected in my performance review.

It was clear to me, now, that Soloman and I were polar opposites. He treated his work as a game, sending messages to platoon members like "Let's go A-Team. Let's see how many arrests we can make tonight!" For me, it was people's lives at stake when talking about arrests, not a game.

A few shifts later I took a call and realized I'd need to get a search warrant to seize telephone records from Bell Canada. I'd never done this before and didn't know how. Not wanting to go to Gerald because of the bad vibes there, I went to Constable Stan Wills. He was two years my senior.

He didn't know how either so, after all, we had to go to Gerald's office.

Wills explained the situation saying that as neither of us knew the procedure to get a search warrant, we were coming to him.

Gerald looked directly at me. "You should know by now how to do a search warrant." He turned away and explained the procedure to Wills, not once making further eye contact with me.

I was furious. He cut me down in front of Wills who had two more years on the force than me but never making the point that Wills should have known, too.

We thanked him civilly as we left, but inside I was fuming.

I could feel it now. I was a walking target. Both Soloman and Gerald had it in for me.

It was no surprise to me when I got my performance review a couple of months later that it was poor. It was the first poor one I'd received since joining Gloucester three-and-a-half years ago. It was filled with statements like: needs more supervision than normal, needs to be more assertive.

I knew I could dispute it if I wanted, but thinking it through I realized I'd be blackballed even further. So I tucked my chin in, straightened my shoulders, accepted the review and carried on. In my naiveté (which I was quickly losing), I considered it testing even though I knew the guys didn't get tested in the same way.

Was this the best thing to do then? It's something I still think about. I thought I could see a pattern of bullying but I was still new on the force, I had just started a relationship that I found fulfilling and supportive, I was only 27, and wanted to succeed at this job.

Soloman, however, was furtively working away in the background sniping at me, talking about me, ensuring I didn't get any notification or praise. I could see it but didn't want to make waves because I knew Soloman would be my Sergeant some day.

I continued to work hard. Soloman continued just as hard thwarting me at every turn, running to Gerald about everything I did, watching every move I made. He told platoon members about every little mistake and it wasn't long before I was ostracized not just by my platoon but I could see and feel ripples throughout the organization. New officers didn't want to ride with me, take calls with me or work with me. They all steered clear, and because Gerald backed Soloman I was seen as a problem.

I was isolated.

The more I tried to get along, the harder they were. Even at lunch other officers grabbed the remote and switched channels daring me to object. I was more than sad, I felt defeated. I didn't know why this was happening.

I hated going to work, I cried in front of my friends, snivelled to my parents and told everyone I wanted to quit. Every day I walked on eggshells wondering if those I said hello to turned around and stabbed me in the back. I didn't trust anyone, felt horrible inside and second-guessed my every move.

All of this was compounded one afternoon when Constable Nic Flagherty was looking for an officer to help on a drug call. I volunteered, and dispatch sent me the call. When I got there I realized there were a whole lot of other cruisers there, all waiting and watching to see what was going to happen. Flagherty gave me a look which blatantly said to get back in my cruiser and leave. I got the not-so-subtle hint, loud and clear; they didn't want me there. As I was leaving, a zone officer who'd been on a towed-vehicle call, radioed and asked if I would tow the vehicle for him. "Sure," I thought. "Why not...I'm just a doormat everyone's walking on anyway." I towed the vehicle.

There were other women on the force now and sometimes I confided in them. We didn't get together often, none of them were on my Platoon and they all had less seniority so the only thing they could do was listen and commiserate. If they spoke up, I knew, and they knew, they'd be blackballed, too; so although they were a good support there was little they could do. My confidence dropped lower and lower each day and Soloman waited patiently like a large spider for me to make a mistake.

I carried on for two more years but everything was wearing thin. One day, a spur-of-the-moment decision took me into Inspector McDonald's office. I always had great respect for him, and when he greeted me with a smile and a 'come on in' I took a deep breath and launched into my story. I told him everything, poured out my heart.

He sat and listened, saying he'd heard some of this, but nothing like I was telling him. I left his office feeling better than I had in years. He told me he'd look into a transfer.

And I did get a transfer a few months later to the Community Service Office. I was going to teach in schools and host safety events for the public. At last I was looking forward to something and especially to turning over a new leaf.

All this time Murray was by my side, listening, drying tears day after day and supporting me. Early on we'd agreed not to fight each other's battles; if Murray had a problem he'd have to fix it, and the same went for me. We were there to be sounding boards and support systems when it came to work but didn't get involved with each other's work problems. We understood each other's issues, complications and problems and the personality types of the people involved. The days and hours we spent together drew us close. We were truly in love and I was profoundly grateful for his support.

— 6 —

A Fresh Start and a Wedding

I received my transfer to the Community Service Section (CSS) in the summer of 1987. This was going to be a new learning experience and I was excited. I had a new Sergeant, new people to work with and a new outlook. After the bullying, sniping and nastiness I'd been through, I felt this was a good place and a new beginning.

The Community Service Section was small; there were six Constables and one Sergeant. This was good. I could get to know the officers and they could get to know me. I hoped they would put aside anything they'd heard and we could start fresh. I was looking for new faces, new friends and a happier life.

In the CSS, each officer made his/her own schedule. Some days we worked afternoons and other days we worked day shift. There were no night shifts or weekends, which was wonderful, a first for me.

As a School Resource Officer I had to go into schools and teach Kindergarten to Gr. 12 students either safety or law. All lesson plans were age and grade appropriate. For example, the Gr. 6 lesson plan on Values, Influences and Peers (VIP) was quite involved. VIP was six lessons and I visited each Gr. 6 class six times. I had 23 schools and each school had to be given fair and equal treatment. Because it was August and the schools were out for the summer, I had a little time to prepare. As well as teaching law and safety, I had to set up displays, plan and run bicycle safety rallies in the spring. Through this section other familiar programs such as Neighbourhood Watch, Block Parent, and Home Security were run. Officers were invited to attend functions and she or he was assigned accordingly.

I took my schools on with enthusiasm. One of the best things about my new position was seeing the other side of life. Instead of constantly dealing with the bad, I met and dealt with the good. It was refreshing; I liked the kids, I liked the teachers and along the way, I learned that some of my Gr. 6 students were sons and daughters of Ottawa officers. Years later I found out that some of those students went on to become police officers themselves because I had an influence on their lives. This was a great morale booster.

Not only did I enjoy what I was doing at work but things at home were busy and exciting, too. In the spring of 1986

Enjoyable years as School Resource Officer

A Fresh Start and a Wedding

Murray and I took a vacation to England and Scotland. While in London, we picked out an engagement ring and four days later, in a tiny little pub in Scotland called The Southern Cross, Murray proposed to me. I wasn't caught entirely unaware but the reality of the proposal brought tears to my eyes. Of course I said "Yes!" when he proposed, and then burst into tears! The gay couple and their dog sitting next to us, as well as the bartender, heard the proposal and I'm sure it was the highlight of their evening, as well as ours. We set a date to get married the following June.

A few officers asked to see my ring when we returned but our engagement was taken pretty much in stride. I settled into my new position and work moved ahead. Some officers were transferred out while new ones transferred in. It's always good to get new blood on a team but I thought these particular new officers were rude and wasn't too impressed. They undermined the team.

The two were Constables Bruce Duff and Patrice Roches. They were pretty much a tag-team and went everywhere and did everything together. Over the months, after listening and watching, I began to see that Roches was a male chauvinist. He continuously made snide comments about women and found fault with them. He compared women police officers on television to the women officers working with him and said things like "Police women (PW) on TV are always dressed in tailored uniforms and well developed; our uniform does nothing for our police women!"

One day, sitting at his computer, he asked "If women are equal to men, why is there a minimum in the slo-pitch event?" And during a sectional meeting, when it was my turn to speak, Roches continually interrupted and joked around with others completely drowning me out. I felt his rudeness made what I had to say of little importance.

In another sectional meeting the topic of women in the workforce came up. Roches scornfully commented that, "It takes two women to make up one man for anything anyway."

Duff, although he was with Roches most of the time, was not as derogatory or disrespectful. But he did laugh along when Roches made stupid comments.

Most police cruisers are air-conditioned but we had one in our fleet that wasn't. One really hot summer day I went in for my shift and saw that all the air-conditioned cars had been claimed. The only one left was the one without air-conditioning.

Knowing that Duff and Roche did everything together, when I found out they both had cars, I asked Duff if he would switch with me. With no hesitation at all, he told me he had errands to run and had to go to Headquarters, so I knew he wasn't going to give up his car.

"Never mind. I'll drive the one with no air-conditioning."

Suddenly I was whacked in the chest by a set of keys — the keys to the non-air-conditioned car. Duff had lobbed them at me with no warning. I was dumbfounded! But, being me, I took the keys and left the office.

There was a moment, later in the day, after lectures and school visits were over, that Duff approached my desk and mumbled a sort of apology.

"I'm feeling bad about hitting you with the keys." He didn't ask if I was okay, or how my day had been, just a muffled, awkward teenagerish apology.

June 6, 1987 arrived. It was our wedding day. The day started off cloudy but by 1600 hours, just in time for vows, the sun shone. We were married at the First Presbyterian Church in Brockville. I'd grown up in this church and it had always been my dream to be married there.

A Fresh Start and a Wedding

Our wedding day — June 6, 1987

Murray hired a neo-classic Excalibur car to drive us from the church to the reception. As we left the church our hand-picked Guard of Honour — Constables Stan Wills, Bernard Partiage, Tim Buchanan and Denzel Turquoise — lined up on the stairs in their dress uniforms. It truly was beautiful. We felt proud and honoured. I was a little teary. We had pictures taken across the street at Court House Square and eventually made our way to the reception overlooking the St. Lawrence River.

We had a great time, and so did everyone else; we were the last to leave, heading to a hotel in Brockville for our wedding night, and then, the next morning returning home to Osgoode. Before we left for our honeymoon we spent a week at home and then left for a further two weeks cruising in the Mediterranean. Murray had travelled his whole life but had never been on a cruise and I'd always dreamt of a cruise for my honeymoon. We travelled on a Greek cruise line and stopped in at 10 ports of call. The weather was fabulous; everything about the cruise was perfect. We enjoyed every minute of our honeymoon. But, all good things must come to an end, and we had to return to work. I, especially, was not looking forward to it.

As time passed, I realized I was no further ahead than when I'd come off the road. The officers continued to ridicule me and made it clear I wasn't one of the team. I felt both unwanted and alienated; I found myself spending as little time in the office as possible, leaving for my schools early in the morning and only returning to drop things off at night. By not being there I wouldn't have to endure being patronized. So much for starting fresh and turning over a new leaf....

One day on my way out to my cruiser, I saw a van blocking the exit. I piled my things into the car and pulled in behind the van noticing at the same time that things were being taken from the van and loaded onto a trolley, so I knew I'd have to wait a bit.

Flagherty was watching. "Honk your horn," he yelled. "Honk your horn."

I ignored him and waited. I could see the unloader was busy.

"Honk your horn," Flagherty yelled again.

I continued to ignore him and instead turned my cruiser around to leave by the other exit. As I passed Flagherty, I could see him shaking his head.

"No balls, no balls," he muttered.

Two-and-a-half years passed and I realized I was getting bored repeating the same lecture at each school. I didn't want the students to be on the receiving end of this, so asked for a transfer back to the road or to a detective's office. I got my transfer but had to finish the year before heading back to A platoon in the lower end of the city. Once again I was patrolling Beacon Hill, zone 212.

—7—

Back to the Road

I was back on shift and working the road. And, just as I'd feared, Soloman became my boss. He was working in the Acting Sergeant position and I had to report to him directly. When someone works in an Acting capacity, it means they are not fully confirmed in that role. They can act for a period of time and then go back to their previous rank, or get confirmed in the acting rank.

I kept a low profile. I didn't want to give Soloman any reason to pick on me.

One night shift Soloman stopped an impaired driver. He arrested him and called me to complete the paper work. He tended to do this a lot; most of the officers talked about it and weren't impressed.

Several weeks passed and I was unenthusiastic about work. I didn't feel welcome by the Platoon and was constantly under scrutiny from Soloman. One night shift, several cars, including mine, were dispatched to a tiny restaurant in the Navan area.

Information was that Popey LaFrenier, a well-known criminal, was throwing furniture around and smashing things.

LaFrenier was a husky guy with lots of tattoos. Five cruisers arrived, and because it was my zone, I went to talk to the restaurant owner; he didn't want to press charges. So I left.

As I headed back to my car I could hear LaFrenier swearing at the other officers; I saw him standing there, fists clenched, asking for a fight. They jeered at him, told him he couldn't drive because he was drunk, but as soon as I told them the restaurant owner didn't want to press charges, they left.

I suddenly realized I was alone in the parking lot with a really angry, belligerent man; he was still yelling, cursing and threatening to get in the car and drive away. I was really pissed off that the others had left me with this raving lunatic and at the same time was thinking back to all my training in how to get out of this situation without horrible repercussions.

I stepped back when he came at me but eventually, with a lot of talking and coaxing, I talked him into taking a taxi home. Dispatch called the taxi, I put him in the car and finally took a deep breath. When I saw it heading out, I took another deep breath.

Before, I was just plain scared. Now I was angry — angry that my Platoon had left me there, alone, to deal with a drunk, raging man in an empty parking lot.

What were they thinking? I'd never do that! Why did they? If things had gone wrong, I could have been punched, kicked, even worse.

Was there any recourse, I wondered?

"Should I tell the Sergeant?"

After thinking this through, I decided it wouldn't get me any further ahead, so I didn't. I wrote my report and cleared from the call.

But the incident did take me back to Use of Force training. Use of Force is mandatory for each and every police officer and it has to be done annually; it's legislated through the Provincial Government. That situation made me sit back and think through what my options were if I had had to use force on Popey. I wouldn't be able to fight as he outweighed me and was twice my size. I could use my baton, pepper spray or my gun but in this particular situation I felt as long as I kept him talking he'd eventually do what I asked…and that's exactly what happened. Communication is normally the best way to de-escalate most situations, although it doesn't work all the time. You really have to think on your feet, assess the situation, plan and then act keeping in mind that you're always accountable for your actions.

Qualifying for Use of Force

Six months passed and although things on the road weren't great, my home life was. I was pregnant! I told Soloman. I was taken off the road and assigned to the front desk in the upper end. There I stayed for the duration.

I was pleased how quickly administration dealt with my pregnancy. An Ottawa officer, when she learned she was pregnant, had to quit her job; they wouldn't accommodate her by taking her off the road. This officer, after her pregnancy, took the Police Force to court to get her job back. I was thankful I didn't have to deal with that.

I enjoyed my pregnancy — no morning sickness and healthy throughout. I worked until Amanda was born in July of 1991. With six months maternity leave and four weeks of annual leave to look forward to, I put my worries on hold and enjoyed my new family.

The months flew by and I returned to work. I was blue about going back. Not only did I have the same old problems, but now I had a little girl to worry about. It was one thing when it was just me and Murray, but now there were three. Safety suddenly became a much more important factor.

In January 1992 I was assigned to F Platoon, working zone 214, which was the Blackburn Hamlet area of Gloucester. My Sergeant was Sgt. Gerald. Not even back two months and I had two complaints filed against me, one from Sgt. Joel Scissons and the other from a member of the public.

The public complaint didn't bother me as much as the one from Scissons. I expected complaints from the public because I knew as long as I worked I was bound to get some. But I didn't expect co-workers to complain about me.

The public complaint was from a driver I had ticketed after a motor vehicle accident; the charge was 'left turn not in safety.' I explained to the driver at the time that, if she wanted to, she could contest the traffic offence in court. She did.

The next time I saw her was in traffic court two months later. I won. The conclusion was that I had properly followed procedure and issued the correct provincial offence notice. The file was closed.

The complaint by Scissons was one I didn't expect. I'd responded to a robbery during night shift a week before Scissons filed his complaint. Information we had was that the cigarettes, balaclava and jacket worn by the suspect were on the penthouse level of the building. I pressed the button to the penthouse level and when the door opened three girls, between five and eight perhaps, were standing there. I guessed they lived in the building because they were running around in T-shirts and it was the middle of winter. They were excited and having fun, jumping on and off the elevator.

As the elevator went up, one of the girls opened her hand and showed me a dime. She said that she'd found it on one of the floors and asked if she could keep it. I didn't know why she shouldn't; as far as I knew it had nothing to do with the robbery. The kids got off the elevator on the 9th floor and I continued to the penthouse.

Sure enough, there were the balaclava, jacket, loose cigarettes and some change lying on the floor. I seized the items and went down to the first floor to speak with the complainant.

While there I noticed a young mother holding a baby; I commented that I'd just returned to work from maternity leave and my baby girl was seven months old. I asked more questions about the robbery and once I had all the information, I went back to the cruiser, wrote my report and left. The robbery was assigned to Scissons for further investigation.

So this is what Scissons said in his complaint...that I was more interested in the baby than about gathering evidence. He was also upset that I told the little girl she could keep the dime, and that the complainant had several packages of cigarettes in her possession and I didn't seize them. I didn't know she had cigarettes, so I didn't take them.

As a result, an informal discipline note landed on my performance appraisal, and Gerald spoke to me about it. He retired several months later and Soloman, once again, became my confirmed Sergeant. Twelve years later I learned that Soloman at that time told the boys in the locker room "...We have to get rid of her..." — meaning me.

I was in for the fight of my life and, as yet didn't realize it. Each and every call I went on, Soloman watched and found fault. He was in a position of power and made my life miserable. It was all in his plan to get rid of me.

Soloman had me under a microscope. I found myself walking on eggshells, even second guessing my own work and all the decisions I made. I was so tense and stressed that twice within a month I slept in and eventually succumbed to the flu.

In April of 1992, Soloman asked me why my work performance was so poor. I was outraged, my insides roiling, thoughts dancing around inside my head. "Maybe if you left me alone, I might have some breathing room," I thought, not speaking. He asked if I had personal problems and suggested I take time off to sort things out. He also said to keep in touch with him during my time off, which I found strange.

I was furious. The only issue I had was my boss!

But I did take time off to collect myself and get an expert opinion on my state of mind. James Bimock was a psychiatrist and a friend, and I thought he might have some suggestions for me. We had one meeting. When I told him what was happening, what I was going through, his immediate reaction was "You're dealing with an asshole." He didn't dwell on it, though, and immediately moved to "…when are you and Murray coming for dinner?"

Reflection tells me he could have taken this a bit further. He didn't suggest I see anyone else, he didn't offer any other sessions. He obviously felt this was good enough. I did go a couple of years later to speak to someone at the Employee Assistance Program (EAP) because Solomon was in my head all the time — at dinner, during the day, everywhere. This counsellor had a simple solution. "Picture yourself ripping his face off," he suggested. I laughed because I'm not a violent person but when the time came, I did just that. What a feeling of relief! I visualized his face coming off in handfuls, and actually burst out laughing right in Soloman's face. Soloman, being the egotistical man he was, would never have understood I was laughing at him and his visualized face dismemberment.

It totally helped me.

But at that time, in my innocence, and as a good employee (doing what I was told), I did as Soloman asked and called regularly to keep him updated. I told him I'd gone to see a psychiatrist and what his name was, and it was only much later I realized Soloman was keeping notes of everything I told him to eventually use against me.

I went back to work three weeks later. That night a call came in about a domestic and I went to meet the woman at the gas station next door to the police station. By the time I got there, the attacker had left, so I spoke to the woman and took a statement: she'd been assaulted by her boyfriend. He'd punched her in the head and face and I could see a large red welt on her left cheek.

I sent out a broadcast that the boyfriend was wanted for assault and within half an hour heard he was seen across the street from the gas station in a fenced-in bus compound. I knew there was no way out other than climbing an eight-foot fence. Soloman asked officers to surround the compound in case he climbed, and he and several other officers went in.

There were continuous up-dates over the air — the man was seen running into a bus, then behind a bus, then underneath a bus. Suddenly the on-air squawk said the guy had climbed over the building, jumped to the ground and was running towards the motel a few hundred yards away. Officers surrounded the motel, checked the restaurant and lobby and ran behind the building where a creek followed the west side. Soloman told the night clerk to lock the door so he couldn't run back inside.

I heard Soloman ask all officers their locations and then told me to move back to the street. Next thing I heard the guy was running towards the street and right at me. I could see Soloman running after him full tilt and figured I'd better start running to keep up. In full pursuit we ran across the street and that's when the runner tripped, tumbling to the ground. Soloman tried to get over him but stumbled and went down, too. I jumped on the runner, and we cuffed him. Soloman looked at me, panting, and said with scathing criticism, "I didn't know if I could count on you for back up."

I was dumbfounded, startled, shocked, and once again furious.

"And who did you think would back you up," I hissed at him, out of breath myself.

That was the longest foot chase I'd been involved in — an hour-and-a-half. The guy was arrested and processed for assault.

The next night during line-up Soloman handed me a phone message from Vince McMahon (owner of the World Wrestling Federation); please call. He wanted me on his tag team. I laughed, had a good giggle at the silliness of it all, only to be told the next moment that Soloman asked me to stay behind after line-up. Oh God, I thought. What now?

Soloman told me I was being sent to The Ontario Police College for the Advance Patrol Course, a refresher course for veteran officers. It was two weeks long and I was scheduled to leave next week. I dreaded going and leaving my family behind. Was this all part of Soloman's plan to get rid of me, I wondered.

A week later I left for OPC. I called home daily to see what was new and to let them know I loved them. I finished the two week course with 93 percent and even though that was a good mark I knew it was back to the horrible reality of life on the road. When I got back, Soloman told me I'd be working the upper end.

Back to the Road

In October 1992 I was working night shift and the weather was cold, foggy and misty. Dispatch sent me on a call to the deep dark rural area of zone 104. Information was that a vehicle was in the ditch and no one had been seen leaving.

I found a half-ton truck ditched on the north side of the road. The driver had hit a driveway culvert and the front end was smashed. Headlights were still on and there was someone inside.

Suddenly the night became ominous. The driver wasn't moving. My heart was pounding as I headed towards the truck.

"Is he dead?" I wondered. "Is he unconscious?...injured... dangerous?"

The window was down on the driver's side and there was a large male inside. His eyes were closed. He didn't seem to be breathing. He had a gash on his forehead and was bleeding from the mouth.

I slowly reached in to check his pulse, my heart pounding even harder. Exactly at that moment Soloman's voice boomed over the radio. "Check for presence of alcohol." I jumped, cursing him. I finally found a pulse and started yelling at the man in the truck. With a lot of shaking he eventually woke up. I could smell alcohol, his speech was slurred, and his eyes glassy and bloodshot. There was little doubt he was impaired so I arrested him, called for back-up and took the man back to the cell block. I processed him there and he was released with a court date.

A few months passed. It was the beginning of 1993. Soloman hadn't eased up on me, keeping a sharp eye on me at all times. He pulled me into his office one afternoon and asked how things were going. I said I thought things were going smoothly and asked him why he'd asked.

He gave me my performance appraisal for 1992. It was bad, as I knew it would be, and I felt sick. I refused to sign it.

Suddenly, the light went on. I realized what Soloman was doing. For the first time, I clued into his plan — the suggested time off back in the spring, his request to call him while I was off, the bad performance review. He was using his position in the police force to compel me to quit, or prepare a case for my dismissal.

After he gave me my performance appraisal, he told me he thought I was a "shit cop and perhaps I should have been a social worker, or something to do with children." And then he had the gall to tell me to take time over my days-off to think about a rebuttal.

He told me when I came back I'd be working the Information Desk because he wanted me to be working in a stable work environment. He also strongly suggested I seek professional help to sort through my issues. Again, I couldn't believe what was happening. I felt sick, angry, intimidated, and wondered where to turn.

I talked it over with Murray in the next four days and decided to take a stand. I began to gather information for my rebuttal by going to records and getting a list of every call I'd taken from January 1 to December 31, 1992. This gave me the type of call and the case number. I went through my court cases and convictions and found incidents where I'd done a good job, including a murder; not one of these had been mentioned in my appraisal.

I took time to think through and write down why I believed my appraisal was not accurate, including things like lack of experience, token female, emotionally and mentally abused, a supervisor who belittled me, and a transfer to Community Service Section. I prepared my written rebuttal carefully and thoughtfully and asked Murray to read it over to make sure it was presented professionally.

Returning to work Monday morning, I reported to the Information Desk as asked. I put my rebuttal in an envelope and sent it off to Inspector Pierce Sockett. A performance appraisal is normally signed off by the Sergeant and the Staff Sergeant assigned to the platoon; if there's a problem, an Inspector will review it.

Inspector Sockett received the rebuttal and prepared a memo for Inspector Borke who would mediate Soloman and I. Sockett was a member of the ol' boys' network and always supported them. In his memo he said my rebuttal was "unclear" and commended Soloman for taking "a problem solving approach." If he hadn't, he added, my performance issues would never have come to light. And he went on to state that I had not brought any problems to the attention of any supervisor with the exception of Inspector McDonald — and that was well after the fact.

I suppose I could have expected a fairer evaluation but was not surprised when he sided the way he did.

Three weeks passed. I was working the Information Desk on midnight shift. At about 0200 hours the front door of the station burst open and Soloman walked in. My stomach turned, I began to sweat and my heart pounded. He came straight through the door leading to the Information Desk, walked around and sat on the other side. He didn't take his coat off so I knew this would be a short stay. "The Inspector received your rebuttal and wants to talk to us about it. It will probably be sometime next week."

"That's fine," I said.

"What do you think you're going to accomplish by all of this," he asked.

"I'll talk about it with you when the Inspector is present," I answered.

He leaned forward, looked me straight in the eye and said, " I think you're sick."

I looked at him, turned away and didn't respond. Soloman left.

I took a deep breath. "How can he get away with this?" I asked, beside myself. "He's driving me insane."

I talked it over with Murray the next day. He listened, encouraged me to stay strong and wait until I could talk things over with the Inspector. That was a difficult weekend to get through; I worried and mulled it over every minute of every day.

Back to work on Monday day shift, Soloman called and said the Inspector would meet with us Wednesday at 1400 hours. Inspector Borke invited us in and the first thing he said was he had a vested interest in this hearing as he had hired both of us. He said he knew we disagreed on many issues, including my performance appraisal, and had called the meeting to clear the air. He asked Soloman to begin.

Soloman told the Inspector he'd written most of his version in memos to his Staff Sergeant. He re-iterated all the negatives in my performance appraisal. He said he was spending hours collecting and writing information for his superiors. He said he'd tried to help me by sending me to OPC on the Advanced Training Course, by placing me in the upper end and then on the Information Desk for a more stable environment. Regardless of what he'd done, he said, my performance remained unchanged and was poor.

It was my turn. I quietly offered the reasons I was rebutting the appraisal. As far as I was concerned, Soloman had not been fair in my assessment; he'd only written negative comments and hadn't ever offered any praise where praise was due, like the murder investigation where I'd put in my own time.

I spoke about Soloman's daily attitude towards me, how he kept me under a microscope and on a short leash so I felt I couldn't breath. He told me I was a "shit cop and should have been a social worker or something to do with children," I told the Inspector.

I said I had zero confidence in any Supervisor dealing with any issue I might have, and gave, as an example, the incident of the search warrant and Sgt. Gerald.

I told him about the incident at the restaurant where I was left on my own to deal with an angry and belligerent Popey Lafrenier and that I felt my colleagues had abandoned me. I added that, in my opinion, they probably didn't have any recourse either as they were all under Soloman's supervision.

I talked about the drug squad asking for assistance in my zone but, in fact, it was me who ended up leaving when all the other officers arrived.

I talked about my attendance record and that not once had I slept in over my 10-year career but under Soloman's supervision I'd been late twice because of stress. And, I told him Soloman had called me "sick."

I said I hadn't been given the opportunities to do special projects, go on courses or move into detective work as those less senior than me had.

I told him I'd been harassed by Soloman and it deeply affected my ability to work.

Then I suggested I be transferred to another Platoon under the supervision of another Sergeant. I said this would go a long way to alleviating my stress, and I was positive my performance would pick up. And, if this could happen, I would work hard to regain my confidence.

Inspector Borke didn't think long. "If we accommodate you and give you a transfer to another Platoon, would that satisfy you with regards to harassment?"

I agreed I'd be satisfied as long as I didn't have to work with

Soloman, and I wanted it acknowledged in writing by the Police Service that Soloman had harassed me and because of that my work performance had been affected. That way, if there were future events, it would show a pattern in Soloman's behaviour, and would not reflect on me or other women down the road.

As quickly as that, the meeting was over. Borke told me the transfer would take a couple of weeks and he would submit a memo to Deputy Chief MacKigh regarding the outcome. He assured me I'd get a copy.

I left the meeting feeling now the Police Service knew Soloman had been harassing me. They wouldn't have offered a transfer so quickly otherwise, I reasoned; it wasn't a normal procedure to do so. Also, Borke focussed on ensuring I was satisfied with the outcome of the harassment part of the meeting.

Within a few days I received a copy of Borke's memorandum to Deputy Chief MacKigh. Nowhere did it acknowledge Soloman's harassment. It was broken into two areas: 1) Performance Appraisal and 2) Harassment and Discrimination in the Work Place.

Borke said he "was not satisfied that the performance problem(s) had been accurately identified" and therefore recommended that they be identified and an action plan be implemented that could be measured as well as monitored. Secondly, he stated "he had no doubt Pam felt she had been harassed and discriminated against."

As far as I could see this was a cover-up, a slick gloss-over of what had happened. By not naming Soloman he got off scot-free.

My self-confidence and self-esteem zoomed to the depths.

Borke further stated it was "imperative the matter be

reviewed within the context of the Police Services Policy on Race Relations, Human Rights and Harassment." He said he would meet with me again to ensure the allegations had been resolved to my satisfaction, or, to give me a choice of having the Professional Standards Bureau or an outside agency investigate the matter.

Borke did meet with me a couple of months later to make sure I was satisfied. By then I'd been moved to a new Platoon and the only thing I wanted was get on with my life. I'd spent way too much time and energy on Soloman. So I told Borke the allegations had been met to my satisfaction.

— 8 —

Not Out of the Woods Yet

In early 1994 I wasn't feeling good about myself and just wanted to move forward. I kept plugging away at work but could feel my self-esteem dropping lower and lower and my sense of security had pretty much reached zero. Soloman was watching everything I did and scrutinizing every decision I made, yet again.

On the up-side, I liked my new Sergeant and was comfortable with my new Platoon members, especially Constable Keith Morrow. But after a month of settling in, there was another change — my Sergeant was re-assigned and another Sergeant joined the Platoon. He would take over the action plan to get my work performance back on track. So much for feeling comfortable!

His name was Nelson Pickford, he was a slender man, used soft tones and had a mousey voice; he was also good friends with Joel Scissons. This immediately caught my attention. He'd probably heard about the complaint Scissons had filed against me and it made me wonder if he could be objective in his dealings with me.

Months went by. I kept busy in my own zone and met with Keith for coffee whenever I could, talked to him about work issues and my home life. I'd known him for about eight years, he was at my wedding, he was married with two children and he'd been at our house for dinner several times. I really liked him, felt comfortable with him. We'd become good friends over the years.

But not long after Pickford came to the Platoon, Constable Percy Honeycomb began to stir the pot. Honeycomb was a big man, not the brightest guy in the universe, but got along with the 'ol boys, including Soloman. He always joked about making his prisoners "lick the stick" meaning all they had to do was look at him sideways and that was enough excuse for him to beat them up.

Once, when I had a 16-year-old in custody for theft, Honeycomb and another officer wanted to interview him because they thought he might be involved in other crimes they were investigating. I agreed, but not very willingly, and when they locked the door with me on the outside, I was furious. I could hear Honeycomb beating the kid. I yelled and yelled and finally, when they unlocked the door, I yelled again and told them never, ever, to do that to a prisoner of mine.

Honeycomb laughed and said we had to get together on our notes, as if he automatically expected me to corroborate with him. More and more I found what I was seeing and hearing harder to take.

Honeycomb was a real pig. On another occasion I knew I had a long night ahead of me so I took a lunch and left it in the refrigerator at the station. When I finally had some free time and could get a bite to eat I headed back to the station only to see Honeycomb coming out of the door with my cookies stuffed in his mouth! When he saw me, he laughed, spewing crumbs down his front. I just shook my head in disgust. He hadn't taken anything else but I didn't want my lunch now that he had pawed it over.

Not only was Honeycomb a pig, and ignorant, he was complaining to other Platoon members, as well as the Sergeant, that I was spending too much time at the station. Because of this, he said, he was taking calls in my zone, and didn't like it.

I knew he was complaining about me; I didn't think about it much. I certainly had the right to be at the station to complete my reports because there were no in-car computers at that time. But it got to the point where he was making my life miserable. One day I complained to Keith explaining that the only reason I was at the station was to write reports.

One evening, when I was off with the flu, Pickford called a Platoon meeting. Platoon members spent the meeting complaining that I was always in the station and they were tired of taking calls in my zone.

Pickford, however, had done his own research. He told them that over the past three months I had taken three times as many calls as any other Platoon member. The reason, he said, I was in the station so often was because I was writing up three times as many reports as anyone else. I heard, when I came back, that suddenly the Platoon had nothing to say, Pickford dismissed them and they returned to the road.

I was hopeful this might be the beginning of change, but it wasn't. Honeycomb kept finding fault with me no matter what I did.

One afternoon I had a new recruit riding with me. While patrolling, there were always lots of messages going back and forth between Platoon members, including Honeycomb. When we got back to the station to write reports, the new recruit started going through messages, and one of them said, "The whale fell in the toilet."

"What?" she asked.

I figured out pretty quickly that Honeycomb hadn't expected me to see this; he'd sent it to everyone else but me. The reference was to me. This was the kind of garbage I experienced on a daily basis.

But topping this indignity was the revelation by the new recruit that Keith was talking behind my back. Everything I said to him he repeated to Platoon members.

I was more than angry; I confronted him. He didn't admit it, but he didn't deny it, either. I was appalled. The one person I thought I could trust betrayed me. Once again I was alone.

What could I do? What should I do?

I did what I had to in order to keep my job, keep my sanity, keep my head above water. I reported for work each day, took calls, and went home.

A few months later Pickford was transferred and Sergeant Nick Flagherty replaced him. He was the guy who used to be on the drug unit, the officer who hinted there were too many officers on scene when the drug squad made a bust in my zone, years earlier. He'd made me feel unwanted then and as I remembered that incident, a lump filled my throat. I suddenly felt myself tensing up. "What am I in for now," I wondered. Flagherty was the third Sergeant to "get me back on track." I really had doubts as to where all this was leading.

This is how I remember Flagherty. He was a vain man; he worked his upper body only and wore his police shirts tight around his biceps to show them off. Murray called him 'chicken legs' because he never worked on them. In plain words, he was all show and no substance.

His style was similar to Soloman's. He was a micromanager — autocratic and manipulative. He watched me like a hawk, and again I felt I was under a microscope, walking on eggshells. I often felt I could hardly breathe. I lost confidence, felt intimidated and belittled, and knew I was fighting a losing

Not Out of the Woods Yet

battle. As long as Flagherty was my Sergeant I knew I could never move forward.

One late afternoon shift around 2030 hours I left for a mischief call at a school in Blackburn Hamlet. When I arrived there was no complainant; I called dispatch. Dispatch said the complainant had waited so long he decided to go to the police station. He was waiting there.

I parked at the front in Visitor Parking when I arrived, looking first to make sure there was lots of parking available. I backed my cruiser into the parking spot and ran into the station; the complainant had been waiting about two-and-a-half hours already. I started taking down the information.

Suddenly Flagherty was on air; in a loud and aggressive tone, he asked who was driving cruiser #33. Dispatch gave him my name.

"Have Cst. Robinson meet me in the parking lot — now!"

Even though the complainant had already waited well over two hours, I left and went down to the parking lot. Flagherty was in a foul mood.

"Move that fucking cruiser now. It's in handicapped parking!" he yelled.

It wasn't, I thought, looking at it. Two wheels were slightly over the handicap line but the majority of the car was in regular parking.

I moved the car as Flagherty angrily strode towards me. He stuck his head in the window and about two inches from my face yelled, "Don't you ever park your fucking car in handicapped parking again! I just gave out two tickets to people parking in handicapped spaces only to come out and see one of our cruisers parked in a handicapped spot."

Needless to say, I was upset but I pulled myself together, and headed back to the station to finish the mischief call. When my shift finally ended, I headed home to tell Murray everything.

But this wasn't the end of it. Two months later, I heard Flagherty talking to another officer. "Well at least I know Cst. Robinson can take the heat." I heard them both laugh. He was referring to the parking event.

This was my thinking: it boosted his ego to see me uncomfortable when he yelled at me, and boosted it a second time bragging about it to a fellow officer. Demeaning me made him feel like a real man.

A week later Flagherty told me to relieve the front desk staff person at Leitrim Station at 1930 hours sharp. I forgot. I didn't remember until 1945 hours when Flagherty came over the air and asked my location.

"I ordered you to relieve the front desk staff at Leitrim at 1930 hours and you're late!"

I immediately turned my car around and headed to the station, arriving ten minutes later. I apologized and remained on the desk for the remainder of my shift.

Months passed; I continued to take calls in my zone. I was gaining experience but never let myself get too comfortable; Flagherty was always there, looming in my mind's eye. I could see signs of improvement despite the micromanagement detailed in my monthly assessments. Slowly I was regaining confidence.

But, unbelievably, once again I heard yet another Sergeant was coming to the Platoon. I couldn't believe it; it was the fourth one in 10 months. He was Shane O'Grady and I didn't know anything about him except that he seemed like a nice man. I hoped this was so.

But four different Sergeants in 10 months getting me "back on track" made me pause for thought; it was disturbing. I saw it as just someone else airing dirty laundry about me which made it "my" dirty laundry. I just wanted to get through this and move on.

O'Grady arrived. I found him pleasant and felt more positive than I had in a long time. My year-end assessment was good and made even better when O'Grady encouraged me to continue working hard.

The year was 1995 and a lot of new changes were coming to the city; three municipalities within the Ottawa region (Gloucester, Nepean and Ottawa) were amalgamating to become one large city and this included all the services joining i.e. Police Forces, Fire Departments, Municipal works. The next few years would be confusing for everyone, but we soldiered on.

— 9 —

A Glimmer of Hope

I continued to work hard over the next three years. I received good feedback from O'Grady with excellent performance reviews. He worked hard to get me into a detective position, but to no avail, so I ploughed through the hardships and physical demands on the road. This was year 14.

In the meantime, Soloman was promoted to Staff Sergeant. And, no surprise to me, he became my Staff Sergeant. I was beside myself. I couldn't escape. Back under his command, once again I was walking on eggshells. I barely spoke to him and very carefully went about my work. He left me alone, surprisingly, and I continued on.

In early spring 1998 I learned I was pregnant again. Immediately I was taken off the road and was happy about this because I knew working at the front desk I would be less likely to run into conflict with Soloman.

Victoria was born in December 1998. I happily took nine months maternity leave and went back to the road in September 1999, back to the zone I'd left behind. All was going well; I had a new Sergeant and Staff Sergeant. Soloman became an Acting Inspector and was working in the east end of the city. My new Sergeant was Paul Flagherty, identical twin of Nick. He wasn't as vain as his brother. My new Staff Sergeant was Peter Hill. He was friendly, liked to laugh and made everyone feel comfortable.

One afternoon Hill called me off the road. When I got to the Station, both Hill and Flagherty were there. I was sure I'd done something wrong but Hill quickly said all was well, he was interviewing Platoon members finding out their five year plans and personal goals.

This was a surprise. I'd never been asked that question before, so I thought hard and fast before answering. But something must have been going on in the back of my mind because I knew pretty quickly what I wanted to say — I wanted experience in investigations, and I wanted to learn more about the promotional process. Some day I wanted to become a Sergeant, maybe even a Staff Sergeant.

Hill asked me what kind of detective work I wanted to do. I said I wanted to learn more about Partner Assault because that was a stepping stone to the Sexual Assault and Child Abuse (SACA) section.

I had gained some investigative skills from being on the road as long as I had — thefts, impaired drivers, harassing phone calls. I'd worked those cases from beginning to end plus others such as robberies, break-and-enters and the occasional murder where I'd completed the initial investigations.

Hill told me he might have some contacts to help me get a detective position and would be in touch when he had some news. I told them how much I appreciated their questions, and thought to myself how different and pleasant it was to have a Sergeant and Staff Sergeant interested in my career and willing to open doors for me.

Several weeks passed. I was asked to get in touch with Inspector Ted A'mour. A'mour asked me to meet him at the downtown station for a get-to-know-you conversation. He offered me a three month stint in Partner Assault and said I would start the following Monday on day shift in civilian clothing out of the downtown station. I was delighted and assured him he wouldn't be disappointed.

Monday came. I started my three month job shadow in Partner Assault. I learned that each officer carried a load of about 50 to 55 cases at any one time. I worked with other Staff Sergeants and Inspectors so they could place a name with a face. I found the experience invaluable and was astonished at how quickly the three months passed; at the end, I went back to the road.

The Staff Sergeant of Sexual Assault and Child Abuse knew I wanted into her section but at that time there were no positions available. I was urged to keep in touch and keep trying.

While I was trying to get a detective position, Soloman was trying to get promoted to Inspector. He took on an Acting position but it was never confirmed. I heard when he was rejected he went back to his office and punched a hole in the wall. He tried a second time and was rejected again. This time he went over to his girlfriend's house and started throwing furniture around. She was pretty scared, and even though a police officer herself, she called the police. Soloman's gun was taken away.

Next I knew, a local paper had latched onto the story asking why this nut bar in the police department held such a powerful position. It went the rounds pretty quickly. I read it and it just confirmed for me who he really was — it painted him in true colours.

Unfortunately, he was eventually promoted to Inspector.

As 2000 approached, I was feeling pretty confident in my work. I made the decision to go ahead with the promotional process. I really had nothing to lose. Administration wasn't helping me move laterally and I could move upward if I passed all the steps. If I passed, that would be great; if I didn't, at least I'd know what it was all about.

The first step was the provincial exam. A pass would make me valid for five years. A pass is 70 per cent. I wrote and passed by two points. I moved on to the interview stage.

It worked like this: in the interview there is a panel of two Staff Sergeants and one Inspector. The questions are behavioural based. They are structured so that if I answered the questions and related them to behaviour, I scored higher. I left the interview thinking I'd done well but wouldn't know the results until the final step, the simulation, was completed. In a simulation, I'd be presented with a situation and have to respond how I would in a 'real' crisis. A good answer meant higher points. I felt good when I finished. Now I just had to wait.

The entire process took about four months. I didn't pass. I was really disappointed. Looking through all my marks I realized the lowest were on the interview so my work was cut out for me next year when I'd try again.

Time passed quickly. A year later I tried again. Even though it was tough to go through it a second time, I felt it was the only way forward.

This time Murray went through it with me; he was aiming for a Staff Sergeant position. We found it easier on the family when we studied and worked together.

I went directly to the second step of the process this time. Throughout the year leading up to this second try, I'd practiced and reviewed how to answer interview questions and felt pretty confident when I left the interview step. The final step was the simulation and, again, I felt good about it.

A Glimmer of Hope

The hard part, of course, was the waiting. This year I passed! Whoopee! Now I could take an Acting Sergeant position or be confirmed directly into a Sergeant's position. At that time there were no Sergeant positions available but that could change within a month or two.

In 2001 I became an Acting Sergeant with my Platoon. I enjoyed the position but found it difficult being an Acting Sergeant one day and then reverting to a position of working with the people I'd supervised the day before.

My first week on as supervisor, I was assigned to a rural area in the east end of the city. It was a huge area; from the most westerly to most easterly point it was about 40 miles. I was working the afternoon shift when I heard cars being dispatched to an area that bordered my boundaries. This was usually covered by another Sergeant, but he was off and I was covering.

Information was that a person had jumped 16 floors. We found a body on the ground and when I felt for a pulse it was clear he was dead.

It was my job to assign tasks as officers arrived; statements had to be taken, the area cordoned off and held for the coroner, the apartment checked and secured, neighbours spoken to, and detectives called in to continue the investigation. It was a busy afternoon.

About a week later, five hours into my shift, I heard cars being dispatched to a motor vehicle accident where the driver had been ejected from the vehicle. It was in a rural area and I told dispatch I would go, too.

When I got there, I saw that a car had sailed over the ditch on the south side of the road and landed on its side in the forested area. The front and back windshields were smashed and the driver had been thrown 20 feet. Officers checked for a pulse and told me he was dead.

Again I put procedures into motion making sure the scene was preserved for the coroner and accident investigators. I really looked forward to my days off at the end of this shift!

I took two days off and returned to night shift. While on a traffic stop I heard dispatchers sending cars to a car fire in the rural area. Although quite a distance from the location, I went to the call. While en route more information came in. There had been some kind of explosion and the fire department was on its way; even more information reported there might be a domestic as well.

When I got there the fire department was putting out a car fire in the lane of a house. A man was arguing with a woman at the end of the lane near a van parked at the side of the road, and a woman was sitting in the van next to the arguing couple. Blood was streaming down her face. The woman in the van was dead, killed by one of the gas-filled shock absorbers located behind the bumper. When the shock absorber exploded from the vehicle it flew down the lane like a rocket through the window of the van killing the woman in the passenger seat and on through the driver's window into the ditch. The male and female arguing had been in the van with the woman. The man was the dead woman's husband; he'd been driving the van. The female was the dead woman's sister; she'd been a passenger. It was a chaotic scene.

I took action and slowly but surely sorted through it, once again securing and preserving evidence for further investigation. It was a tragic situation. The three people in the van were driving by when they observed the car on fire in the lane. It was the dead woman's idea to go back and see if someone needed help. Her husband turned the van around and drove back to the end of the lane where the car was burning. From there, events unfolded.

Who knows why, but I couldn't seem to avoid death on my watch; my nickname became the 'angel of death'.

A Glimmer of Hope

On Patrol

I hoped we'd seen enough death for a while and things would settle down. Day shift went by and all went smoothly; we started afternoon shift. I'd just grabbed a bite to eat when I heard dispatch sending cars to an air balloon accident.

I called dispatch; I was about 15 minutes away and set off with lights and siren. When I got there, the road hadn't been blocked off so I asked for two cruisers, one at each end to block the road and redirect traffic.

This was the scene: people were walking all over, the fire department was there, two men were sitting on the rear of the fire truck, officers were scattered at various locations throughout the scene.

I saw the balloon lying in a field close to the road on the south side. The balloon basket was burnt and a partially burnt body was inside. Officers were keeping a man from running to the balloon. When I arrived I learned that the two men on the

75

back of the fire truck were driving by and witnessed what happened. The man struggling to get to the balloon was the father of the woman in the basket. She was 16 and the father had been the pilot. The mother and a good friend were the ground crew, and were also on scene.

I really had to act fast and compassionately. I assigned officers to various tasks, and as I was doing this, I noticed a woman stumbling through the scene, ranting and crying. I finally reached her only to learn she was the mother of the 16-year-old. I was able to coax her over to the cruiser (to keep her away from the balloon) and asked an officer to sit with her so I could continue to assess and take control of the scene.

Any officer that showed up was put to work. The Duty Inspector arrived and asked for an update. I reported, and then made sure the scene was secure for the aviation people arriving from Toronto in the morning. After it was all over, the Inspector asked me how I felt. Chaotic, intense, terribly emotional, tragic — but we got through it, I said. That seemed to satisfy him.

Later, writing my report, I noticed one of my officers having a hard time. I went over to talk to him; he said he'd never, ever, seen anything like that before. I talked with him for a while and checked in with him a couple of times over the next week to make sure he was moving on (no one had ever checked on me!) He was.

The incident had taken a toll on me, too. When I went home that night, after working overtime, I woke Murray up and told him the whole thing. He listened, comforted, and we talked for awhile. He eventually went to sleep but I stayed awake even though I started afternoons the next day.

It had been a very busy six weeks of my acting position but I took in every detail. A short six months later I was confirmed in that position. I was more than delighted; I was thrilled and happy and proud. This meant I could apply for different positions in the police department.

I filled out all the necessary paper work and then sat back and waited. If a position opened up, I'd be notified.

—10—

Deceived

The week following my promotion I was offered the Administrative Sergeant's position in West Division. That meant I'd have to move from the east end of the city to the west. The biggest incentive was I'd be off the road and finally have an opportunity to build new skills. I was ecstatic. An added bonus was straight days.

Aware that Acting Inspector Soloman was in West Division, I studied the organizational chart before accepting. I didn't fall under his command and so I took the position. I thought if I did have to deal with him, it would be in very small doses.

I had court on Friday and then was heading for a weekend off; the next Monday I'd start my new position. While on my way home my cell phone rang and who should be on the other end than Soloman. Just hearing his voice sent me into panic mode. "Hi Pammy. Nick Soloman here. Are you driving?" I answered yes. "Call me back when you get home, please."

My heart was pounding. A million thoughts rushed through my head and I broke into a sweat.

When I got home I told Murray that Soloman had called. He gave me a hug, told me to calm down, and call him back. I did

The Truth behind the Badge

and couldn't believe what he was saying; there'd been a change in plans, I was going back on patrol where I was needed more, and not only that, it would be under his supervision!

The explanation, according to him, was they no longer needed an Administrative Sergeant and I would be better utilized where they were short — on patrol.

"Whose decision was this?" I asked. Soloman said he'd taken the matter to Patrick Cosby, Superintendent of West Division, and ultimately it was his decision.

To say I was beside myself would be an understatement; I was apoplectic. I couldn't believe this was happening. Adding insult to injury, Soloman told me to report for duty the following Monday, on night shift.

When I got off the phone I tried to reason out why this was so stressful — it was in the west end of the city which I didn't know well, I didn't know any of the other officers, and I was working the opposite shifts of Murray.

The only recourse (as I saw it) was to call the Superintendent; I picked up the phone and placed a call. No answer, so I left a message. Two days later when he called back I asked him point-blank why this particular decision was made — especially when he knew the history between the two of us.

"It's all about numbers, Pam, it's all numbers."

"But if I'm back under his command the problems are just going to continue."

He repeated his first statement. "It's all about the numbers."

So I took a deep breath and told him I wouldn't accept his decision. I'd take it to the Deputy Chief.

"Do what you have to," he said.

I dreaded what was to come but showed up for work an hour

ahead of time at 2000 hours the following day. I realized I knew the other Platoon Sergeant when I arrived, which slightly mollified me. I met Staff Sergeant Brice McDade, the other Platoon members and then it was work as normal.

The west end was busy, there was no down time. My biggest challenge was learning names and how things operated.

But I couldn't get that perverse, out-of-the-blue decision out of my mind. So, on day shift, I went to see the Deputy Chief. I told him I couldn't accept the Superintendent's decision. He agreed to speak to the Superintendent and they'd take it from there.

Superintendent Cosby finally called. His first concern was getting through the summer. "If you can help us with this, we'll help you in the fall with a transfer." I was really unhappy about this request knowing it had come from Soloman, and said as much to the Superintendent.

As time moved on I began to feel more comfortable with my new Platoon. I liked the Staff Sergeant and got along well with him. One night shift I brought him coffee and sat down for a talk. I told him about Soloman and me thinking he might like to know as he was the buffer between us.

Work was going okay when one shift something really odd happened…a commendation showed up in my mailbox written by Acting Inspector Soloman. Immediately my mind backtracked to all the underhanded, manipulative ways he had whacked me in the past.

I was puzzled, but thought I'd hang on to it as I might need it down the road. Within a month three more commendations came my way, all from Soloman. This was truly weird. After telling me just a short time ago I never should have become a cop, he was now saying I was the best thing since sliced bread; this was hard to believe!

After a lot of thought, I realized what Soloman was up to. He was on an upward slope in his career, and in his climb up the ladder his next step was to get confirmed in the position of Inspector. He wanted to prove that he had no problem with female officers, especially me. It would certainly make him look bad if someone complained and he couldn't risk that. By commending me it would keep everything (mostly me) at bay. If something arose in the future, he could fall back on the commendations he'd given putting the blame on my shoulders. I didn't believe a word of the commendations but I hung onto them anyway. It was typical behaviour from Soloman, behaviour that I knew well.

One August afternoon shift, I heard my officers being dispatched to a missing eight-year-old boy call at about 1700 hours. The weather was hot and beautiful so there was lots of light left for searching. I gave the officers time to arrive and get an initial investigation underway. A lot of the time I knew that missing-person calls sort themselves out quickly. After 45 minutes I made my way to the call.

The boy was last seen at his friend's house. When the mother called asking if her son was there, she was told he had left an hour and a half ago; the walk home only took about 10 minutes, so Mom was worried. She contacted other friends where he might have stopped; no one had seen him. This was out of character, according to Mom. He'd never wandered away before.

Officers checked the residence from top to bottom. No boy. I asked for a helicopter and additional manpower to continue the search; I got three more officers and sent them knocking on doors. I walked the neighbourhood as well.

The helicopter was equipped with FLIR (forward looking infrared) cameras and could detect body heat (living or dead). It was dusk so time was of the essence. I asked for a picture of the boy, and the story was on the news. By the end of my shift, the boy was still missing.

I passed information along to the night shift who continued the search; they called in the search-and-rescue team and began to walk a grid. Officers walk a grid-like pattern similar to that on a chart. It was not until 0615 hours the following morning that the boy was found underneath a tarp, asleep, at his friend's house. For some unexplained reason he didn't want to go home that night and decided it was a good idea to sleep under a tarp.

After the boy was found, the search was called off. I learned the news the following day on my afternoon shift and was pleased he was safe and sound.

The month of September was painful. One evening before night shift I felt such an excruciating pain I couldn't even call out to Murray. Eventually it ebbed but we set off for the hospital after getting a babysitter.

A few hours later, after X-rays and an ultrasound, I found out I'd had a gall bladder attack and would have to have my gall bladder out. The hospital would let me know when. A date was made for the surgery but I had to take two weeks to recover. I told the Staff Sergeant so he could make plans.

The night before my surgery, the home phone rang. To my dismay, it was Soloman. He sounded almost compassionate. He said he'd just heard the news and asked if I would ask Murray to call him after the surgery. I said sure, hung up the phone and fumed to Murray. "Why would he do this now? He couldn't care less about me? Why can't he just leave me alone? Calling the night before my surgery just adds more stress."

Murray hugged me and told me not to worry about Soloman. All went well the next day and I was in and out of hospital in about five hours. Murray called Soloman, as requested, and Soloman thanked him for letting him know.

Two weeks later I was back at work; I worked the front desk for the first week back, as I still had a bit of pain and thought my gun belt might sit on the incision. The Staff Sergeant agreed. He was going on holidays and so the other Sergeant agreed to work the road.

The summer passed and I reminded Superintendent Cosby about his assistance with a transfer. He said to leave it with him and he'd get back to me. A few weeks later he called. There was a position in the call centre coming up. He asked if I'd be interested. I was. I just wanted off the road.

I knew the position wasn't a popular one because it involved supervising several female civilian members and there were always issues with sick leave. I'm sure I was offered the position because no one else wanted it but at this point I didn't care, I just wanted to develop new skills. I started in September 2002.

— 11 —

New Skills and a Wide Awakening

I hadn't worked with a lot of civilian members before and was looking forward to it. I'd worked with dispatchers on patrol but never supervised them, or any civilians.

The call centre is really a section for dead-end cases. It's where a lost wallet is reported, but there's no investigation and the report is for information and insurance purposes only.

There were 22 civilian members in the call centre and two supervisory Sergeants. The Sergeants reported to the Staff Sergeant who headed the section. When I entered the section there was only one Sergeant and she was leaving at the end of the month. I was told a second Sergeant would be assigned to the section as soon as one became available. This meant that I had to learn fast as all 22 civilian members would be my sole responsibility for a time.

This was the first time in 16 years that I didn't have to work nights; I worked either days or afternoons. It was also the first job I'd had where I could wear civilian clothing. It was such a treat not to carry the gun belt and bullet proof vest.

I had three weeks to learn how the office functioned as the Sergeant who was training me was leaving to teach at the

Ontario Police College. Three weeks came and went in the blink of an eye.

My new Staff Sergeant, Harry Costello, was a gruff guy; he either liked you or didn't. He was a big man with salt and pepper hair and a beard, and even though he had a deep intimidating voice, I hit it off with him.

A big part of the call centre was the numbers. Each call taker was monitored on the length of time they spent on the phone, how many calls they took during a shift and how many reports they created. Monthly stats were compiled by the Information Technology Centre and sent back to us. These statistics were monitored by the Staff Sergeant and the higher-ups. It was the goal of the call centre to have the calls answered as quickly as possible and not have members of the public on hold for more than 30 seconds. Although this goal had been set four years before my time, it had never been met.

After I'd been at the call centre for about two months, Lou (Sergeant Louise Fossilthwate) arrived as the second Sergeant. She was a great person. She cared deeply about people, was openly gay, was smart and compassionate. She was a large woman with a Scottish accent, short black spiky hair and wore blue-rimmed glasses. I quickly trained her and brought her up to speed on how the call centre worked. We got along really well and actually had fun on the job.

Big gruff Costello, on the other hand, didn't see eye-to-eye with Lou. I suspected he didn't like gay people. For no apparent reason he treated Lou differently than me. He didn't like or accept her ideas and didn't support her in any way. Of course Lou found this frustrating and didn't look forward to facing Costello on a daily basis. She did her best to hide it but I could see how it affected her. I gave her as much support as I could because I had gone through the same crap myself. To make it worse, Costello flirted with me while he was cold-shouldering Lou. He was a pig, like most of them. So Lou and I had a great time when it was just the two of us on together. The days he wasn't there, we felt like celebrating!

Once I'd trained Lou, we split up the shifts into day shift and afternoons; the call centre was supervised for most of its open time from 0700 to 0200 hours.

In February Costello told me he was going away for a three-week holiday and asked me to take over. I said sure and looked forward to proving myself.

We were one week into Costello's vacation when things began to go haywire. I was working day shift and one of the women didn't show up. No message came through saying she was sick, and no message was left on my voice mail. I knew this particular employee was going through a difficult time and there was some concern for her mental health. After calling three times, with no answer, I called dispatch and had a cruiser drop around to check on her.

About 45 minutes later she finally called, madder than hell. She said she hadn't shown up for work because of a late night. "I'll be there as soon as I pull myself together," she yelled, slamming down the phone. "Hmmm," I thought. "Maybe I won't care so much the next time."

Just a few days later I was working day shift again when another employee thought she was having a heart attack. This woman had a reputation for abusing sick leave and we knew she would do almost anything to get out of work. One of the others came to me saying this woman was in distress.

I went to check it out. "How are you feeling?" I asked. She said her breathing was laboured and she felt a tightness in her chest. I asked if she wanted to go to the hospital. "No," she said abruptly. She wanted to go home. I said the hospital would be better, but she refused. "Is anyone at home?" I asked.

Yes, her husband was there. So I drove her home and someone else drove her car. I left her with her husband.

A few days after that there was a power outage. When the power goes out it throws all the phone lines out. There was a back-up system in place but I'd never used it. It was all new to me. Between Lou and me we got things up and running with little down time. I was relieved and mentioned to Lou I couldn't wait until Costello got back so he could put out some of the fires.

When he returned the following Monday, I filled him in on all the happenings. As he listened he rolled his eyes. I could tell he wasn't pleased.

As the days passed I developed a pretty good picture of how the centre worked; on a daily basis three or four people called in sick. It was frustrating but there was nothing I could do — that was for Costello and Health Services to sort out.

It was always the same people calling in. Lou and I knew them well. One of our responsibilities was to complete work assessments for each employee. After we wrote them we sat down with the employee and discussed them. This was really time consuming and we often thought the whole process a sham. Even though we discussed ways to motivate them, we couldn't do it; it had to come from them. We signed and they signed…and they went back to their old ways. If they could screw the system they would. They were just plain lazy. Some days it felt like we were beating our heads against a brick wall but there was nothing we could do. If they were happy with their performance reviews, and had no desire to get ahead, that was it — you can lead a horse to water but you can't make it drink…as they say.

So life in the call centre had its challenges, but overall was fairly good. I was enjoying working days and afternoons and liked my job. I got along well with Costello and Lou, and the

New Skills and a Wide Awakening

majority of the time with the people I supervised. But this was the calm before the storm.

One afternoon shift an employee asked to speak to me. I asked her in and pointed to a seat.

Dana Moore was a good worker, both clear and concise in what she had to say. She launched right in — there was no way to say it tactfully or politely. Ruth Dawson, she said, smelled of (what they thought was) animal poop. Dana wasn't the only one who could smell it but no one else wanted to step forward. They weren't sure what the smell was but were pretty sure it was animal poop.

Dana said each time Ruth walked into the call centre the odour punched her in the nose and it was difficult to work. Ruth sat two rows over and two people in front. If working the same shifts she smelled the smell the whole shift. She said she was lucky she didn't have to share a work station; those who did said it was foul.

A day later, I spoke to Lou about it. Lou, apparently, had also been approached by other staff members complaining of the smell. They actually sprayed their work area with a deodorizer. So Lou and I decided we'd have to bring this to Costello's attention.

We discussed it with him and between the three of us decided to speak to Ruth and offer her some options. But before the meeting I did some homework. I called a veterinarian's office and found out that if there are lots of cats in a house they become stressed and often refuse to use the litter box. I also learned that toms spray their urine and if it gets into carpets or onto furniture no amount of cleaning will get it out. The only way is to remove the carpet. I contacted Pet Smart and got a list of deodorizers and cat litter for pets. So I was prepared for Ruth when she came back to work from two days off.

The Truth behind the Badge

We were really nervous because it was a delicate situation. Really, how do you tell a person in a nice way that they stink? As we headed to the meeting room my heart was beating fast. Before we started I told her our discussion wasn't going to be easy but we had to work out a solution...and then I launched into it.

Some members in the call centre, I said, had told us on several occasions that she smelled, and they said it smelled like animal poop. Before Ruth could say anything, I told her what I'd found out from the vet's and the pet store and then asked her how many pets she had at home. Two cats and three dogs, she said, all litter and house trained. I asked if she wanted to try some of the things I'd learned about — different brand of kitty litter, animal deodorizers. I also suggested she store her clothes away from the pets, maybe in a spare bedroom. I even offered to arrange a second locker at work to keep clean clothes in. I suggested a thorough cleaning/disinfecting of her home and if the carpets were badly soiled and stained that maybe she should get rid of them. I asked her for her own suggestions; she had none. At the end of our discussion I said we would have a follow-up meeting in three weeks to see how things were going, to see if she needed to do anything more.

After three weeks there was no change. We met with Ruth again and she said she was doing everything we'd asked — putting her clothes in a spare bedroom, changing the type of kitty litter, and cleaning it every three days. And then she leaned forward and asked if I could smell anything on her. All I could smell was some type of ammonia.

Because we knew that call centre members were still complaining about the smell, Lou asked if maybe Ruth had a few more animals than she initially admitted. Not at all put out by this, Ruth said she had a lot of dogs; in other words, she'd been lying. But when Lou went over the bylaw about the number of pets she was allowed in the house, Ruth said she didn't live in Ottawa so the bylaw didn't apply to her. We left it at that, agreeing to meet again in a month, with Lou and I wondering just how many animals she did have in the house!

I told my Staff Sergeant what had happened and he suggested I get in touch with both Health Services and the Inspector, if further follow-up was necessary, because he was going away for six weeks.

It didn't stop there. Over the next couple of weeks we continued to get staff complaints, eyes watering from the smell, possible flea bites. Staff brought flea spray to work and asked for deodorizers from cleaning staff. I asked for plastic mats under the chairs to prevent odour seeping into the carpets, and I also asked to have the entire call centre carpet and chairs cleaned. And I took another step; I contacted the municipal bylaw section where Ruth lived. Their bylaw was five animals maximum per household and no more than three dogs. I found out the Humane Society wouldn't interfere unless animals were in distress or injured.

It was just a few days later, on day shift, when one of the staff members started yelling on the phone.

"Ruth, Ruth, breathe sweetie," I heard her say.

I asked to talk to Ruth but was ignored.

"I hope you guys are fucking happy now," she shouted when she hung up.

"They put three of her dogs down."

She was getting up to head over to Ruth's place when I told her, rather forcefully, to sit down.

"I will go!"

Both Bylaw and the Humane Society had been at Ruth's house that morning and had seized many cats and dogs.

Suddenly, after the stress of the morning and the lead-up to it, I felt light-headed. I sat down quickly, stuck my head between my knees and took some deep breaths. Slowly I started feeling better...but I realized this was really getting to me.

When Lou arrived for her afternoon shift, I told her everything that had happened. We had a meeting set up with the Humane Society at 1400 hours and when we got there and saw pictures of the house, we were appalled. There was hair and poop everywhere, no litter boxes, two dead puppies and one barely recognizable as a dog. They seized 38 puppies, six dogs and 10 cats. One dog and all of the cats were put down for distemper. Ruth had been running a puppy mill and the dogs had free rein in the house.

A follow-up visit was scheduled in two weeks with the acknowledgement that if Ruth had the house cleaned the Humane Society would consider returning two dogs and one cat but only if conditions were suitable.

We left the meeting horrified at what we'd been told and doubly horrified that one of our employees was living in those conditions. And I think what surprised us most was the reporting of a foul smell at work had lead to all this....

I wrote a report a few days later and met with the Inspector and Deputy Chief. One result of the whole event was that an internal plan was put in place within the department so that if other situations arose there would be a process and protocol in place to deal with it.

Weeks passed. Things in the call centre settled down and the Staff Sergeant came back from vacation. I filled him in on the happenings over the last six weeks and he was flabbergasted but that didn't keep him from setting another task for us. Heaven forbid we sat still for too long! Our new assignment was to put together interview questions for the hiring of three new call takers. He'd review, and approve, the questions. Once the questions were set, Lou and I would look at resumés, pick out the best and slot them in for interviews; we'd conduct the interviews, grade candidates and recommend if they should be hired. We settled in to our new work.

One day, during this assignment, I ran into Nic Soloman. "So, there's a lot of talk that the Sergeants in the call centre are going to be replaced by civilians," he said. I looked at him, and said, "Just another page in my book Nic, just another page."

Later in the day I asked the Staff Sergeant if this was true. He said yes, and it might happen sooner, rather than later. "Can this be happening again," I wondered. It was probably back to the road for me.

Sure enough, within two weeks Lou and I learned we'd be leaving the call centre and replaced by civilians. To add insult to disruption, we also learned we'd have to train those civilian members coming in. Soloman, I figured, got a certain amount of joy telling me this, a reminder that he was plugged into the network, and I wasn't. And he probably got a vicious thrill that I was being sent back to the road...again.

Lou and I trained the civilian employees in the first week and spent the last week tying up loose ends, getting ready to move. I learned I'd be going back to the road — no surprise there — and wasn't happy. I'd be in the south end of the city where there was lots of gang activity. This was not what I wanted.

During my last week I was working an afternoon shift when I heard one of the call takers say, "Kidnapping, drugs, oh, oh, just a minute please."

The caller said that he and his wife lived in a small village within the city limits and were currently on their way to New York; he was calling the police on his cell phone. He said he thought his children might be in danger and wanted them checked on. The children were at home with their grandmother.

He continued. His wife's brother had been kidnapped along with his girlfriend in Connecticut and had been held captive for two weeks on their way to New York City. The brother was involved in drugs and his captors were also in the drug trade. His captors threatened to harm his family, so that was the reason he wanted his children checked on. Once they arrived in New York, the brother and girlfriend escaped from the apartment where they were being held. They ran to a hospital and notified the New York police from there.

The caller gave me the name of the Inspector and his detachment in New York. I took the information and told him I would check on his kids and get back to him. I telephoned the Inspector in New York and he said it was all correct. He added that the girlfriend had been sexually assaulted several times along the way and her boyfriend had been tortured. I took the information upstairs, spoke to a detective and then put everything in a report for him.

I made arrangements to have a patrol car drive to the residence and check on the kids. They were safe and I called their father.

When my report was finished, I sat back and thought, "You never know what's going to happen in this line of work, even if it's just a phone call."

I went home that night, hugged my children, told them how much I loved them and told Murray the tale of my day.

— 12 —

On the Road Again, with Attitude

Back in uniform and working in the south end of the city where local gangs were fighting over drug territory, call volume was through the roof and officers were run ragged. Once again I was on night shift, one of three Sergeants on F Platoon.

I quickly discovered that not a lot had changed on patrol. There was one thing, however, I'd never seen before — the attitude of younger officers. I knew that officers worked hard but I often felt their egos got in the way of good judgment. I'd

seen a lot of egos over the years but never as blatant as this, particularly in women and new officers. Normally it took a couple of years for the brash ego to raise its head, but not on F Platoon. Female, male, it didn't matter. These officers (with only one or two years under their belts) knew everything there was to know about policing.

I was working a Sunday day shift when an alarm came in. It was in a business area with dozens of businesses. Two officers were dispatched. I heard the officers tell dispatch they had an insecure building. As they checked through the building all was silent on the radio. One officer eventually said all was in order; he asked if a key-holder was available. Dispatch said there was no key-holder on record so the officers cleared from the call and left the building unsecured. I knew this was against policy, and if no one remained on scene, once police were involved the police would be held liable. This could lead to trouble for the officers. As soon as the officers cleared, they were sent to another call.

In order to stave off future problems for them, or the police service, I asked dispatch to send me the particulars of the alarm. I drove to the business, looked for information about the key-holder, found it and made a phone call. Within a half-hour I had the key-holder there and secured the building. I cleared from the call.

When the end of the day rolled around, I went to find and talk to the two officers, a male and a female; I explained that the police could be held liable if the business had been further damaged, or if further thefts occurred because of the unsecured building. Both looked at me as if I had two heads, and said nothing. They did not thank me for completing their job, they did not thank me for keeping them out of trouble, and they certainly never mentioned they would never do it again! I was dumbfounded. I couldn't believe the attitude of these young officers.

On the Road Again, with Attitude

As I continued working with these officers I learned more about each of them, and more about other members on the Platoon. There were others with large egos and I learned quickly that the young men and women marched to the drum of only one of the Platoon Sergeants — and I wasn't the one. This Sergeant could say or do no wrong. I accepted that they saw him as an excellent leader; my problem was that they had no respect for the two other Sergeants on the Platoon, each of whom had his/her own unique experience. They still had to work with us when their favourite was on leave.

About one month into F Platoon, I was invited to meet with the Sergeant and Staff Sergeant in Sexual Assault and Child Abuse (S.A.C.A.). This was exciting news; this was where I had wanted to be for years. The meeting came and went. It was simply to confirm I still wanted to go to the section and to ensure all the correct paperwork had been filed in the event of an opening. I was told if a position became available in the near future, I would be considered.

Life on F Platoon carried on. Some members left and some stayed. In the winter of 2007, during a snow storm one night shift, one of those members who had left F Platoon and transferred to D.A.R.T. (Direct Action Response Team), Constable Dwayne Hallett, came over the air asking officers to get to the area where he was working. No one knew what he was working on, or if he was dealing with individuals that might be dangerous. As the 'favourite' was on leave, I was working the road with the other Sergeant. Several officers, as well as me, started to head to the area in the snow storm. Suddenly I heard that Hallett was in a foot pursuit and heading towards a business area in the south/east end of the City. Within a few minutes I heard the individual was in custody.

I carried on towards the occurrence and as I arrived I noticed an ambulance on scene with the accused inside. I was told that the driver had stopped on route to another call when he saw officers on the same street; he asked if they needed assistance. Hallett told the paramedics that the accused was having difficulty breathing and asked if they could check him out. Hallett had been doing surveillance on the accused as he was in a stolen vehicle and a drug dealer, and I learned that the accused had a long history of faking health issues to avoid police detention.

I watched closely wondering if the person in custody might experience Excited Delirium Syndrome. This is a condition where a person can become agitated, have anxiety, become disoriented, display violent and bizarre behaviour, and have an elevated body temperature. In extreme cases it can result in death by cardiac or respiratory arrest. I asked Hallett if he was going to the hospital with the person in custody. He said he would once he towed the stolen vehicle. He thanked us for our assistance.

Several months later I met Hallett again. A person at a bus shelter was robbed and Hallett and his partner were in the area. Two officers were dispatched and I arrived, too. I saw that Hallett and his partner had arrested and taken the suspect to the ground. One was on top cuffing him while the other stood off to the side. After they got the suspect to his feet and into the police car, witness statements had to be taken and further investigation done. I told Hallett the officers could help with witness statements but any further investigation would have to be done by him and his partner because the other officers had other calls.

It was as though I was talking to a wall! Hallett and his partner ignored me, got into their police cruiser, and left, heading for the police station. I knew if evidence wasn't collected and witness statements not taken, he would not have a case. My officers and I were stuck cleaning up the mess — yet again. I assigned officers to various tasks, got into my cruiser, and I asked Hallett to call me. He called. When I asked why he'd left without completing the investigation he gave me some lame excuse as to why they couldn't do it. I felt he was arrogantly disrespectful and dismissive. I got off the phone, completely frustrated, but feeling there was little I could do. My options were to complain to his supervisor — another male with a large ego — or let it go. In the end, that's what I did. I let it go.

A few months later I was working night shift when several of us were dispatched to a call involving drugs. Information on the call was to meet the complainant as he had information drugs were going to be transported from the west end of the city to his residence in the south/east end. Upon arrival, we met with the complainant. He told us he'd received a call from his 10-year-old daughter. She said that his friend had put drugs into her backpack and was going to bring them back to his residence with him. The complainant wanted police to intervene prior to his daughter and friend arriving at his residence, as he wanted no part of this nor did he want his daughter to be in any type of danger. He went on to tell officers that if they contacted a particular person he could give more specific details about what was to happen.

I asked the other two officers to get a statement from the complainant while I contacted the person for further details. I spent about 45 minutes talking to him. Once off the phone I told the officers what was going to take place and called my Staff Sergeant to update him. I got in touch with West Division to have officers stand by in the event these people went mobile. Once West Division officers arrived, they told me there was no vehicle of that description at the residence and it appeared the people had already left. With this new information I asked my officers if they would go downstairs and move their cruisers, along with mine, so that when the people arrived they would not be spooked. Then it was simply a waiting game.

The complainant's daughter, as well as a male and a female in the vehicle, were expected to arrive within a half hour. We waited in the stairwell. We had a perfect view of the apartment and would have no problem seeing the people enter. About 20 minutes later they arrived. We followed them into the apartment. As it turned out it was only the female and the complainant's daughter who arrived, no male. After questioning the female and searching her backpack, we found no drugs. Information received from her was that the drugs were left in the west end and would be dispersed the following day.

I contacted my Staff Sergeant to tell him the outcome and we discussed calling the drug unit in case they wanted something further done while officers were still on scene. I took the initiative and went ahead and contacted Sergeant Juan Seinfeld. I explained the situation and asked if there was anything further the drug unit wanted us to do while still on scene, as it was the drug unit who would be doing the follow-up. He was flippant and curt. "Well, you're the Sergeant on scene. It's your decision." I was livid. When I offered assistance, this was his answer?! It was typical. Seinfeld was one of the ol' boys and dismissed me with a shrug. With that, I hung up and told my officers they'd done everything they could. I told them to submit their reports to the attention of the drug section. I did the same, and cleared from the call.

I was sick and tired of being everybody's doormat. If it wasn't the young officers, it was the ol' boys. It had reached the point where I had no faith in my administration. All I could do was my job and try and ignore the people who went out of their way to make my life miserable. It didn't matter what rank I spoke to, I always came away with the same feeling that nothing would happen nor did they care. I felt defeated.

After my days off I returned to day shift. When I reported for my shift, the Staff Sergeant called and asked me to report to East Division once I'd completed line-up. Staff told me the

On the Road Again, with Attitude

Superintendent wanted to see me but he didn't know why. After a little tidy-up work I headed off to see the Superintendent. Normally I would have been nervous, but I wasn't this time; he gave me some great news. I was being transferred to Central Division to work in S.A.C.A.

I was ecstatic.

"When?" I asked.

"Immediately...today," he said.

I relayed the news to my Staff Sergeant, spent a couple of hours packing up my desk, obtaining a locker, and then headed for S.A.C.A.

As was typical, when I arrived there was no information about my transfer, so I made myself as comfortable as I could for a while. I wasn't about to complain as this was a position I'd been wanting for about 10 years. But no information could be found so I headed home with orders to report for work at 0800 hours the next day. I left with a grin on my face and a hop in my step.

—13—

A New Experience

It was a bright, sunny day in the spring of 2007. I was in my new office at 0800 hours sharp. It was the second time in my career of 25 years that I could wear civilian clothing. It felt good! I was excited to start my new position as a detective. I'd been waiting for this opportunity for what felt like an eternity.

As I entered the office I saw a few people talking. The Sergeant acknowledged me, pointed, and said, "Just have a seat there Pam. Staff Sergeant Skipper won't be in until about 0900 hours. She'll tell you about your day once she arrives." I took a seat and waited.

It was an open concept office. There were about 14 workstations for detectives and an additional five for civilians. Each workstation had a computer, phone and a divider separating it from the next. The Staff Sergeant's office was at the back and closed-in for privacy. The office had grey carpeting, fluorescent lighting, a microwave and a coffee maker.

I was a bit nervous; I'd investigated thefts, impaired drivers, break and enters and assaults but didn't have any real interviewing skills. And I'd never investigated cases of the caliber I'd encounter in this particular section. Shortly after

0900 hours Staff Sergeant Skipper arrived. She was dressed very conservatively in a navy blue jacket, white starched blouse, grey pants and low-heeled black shoes. She stopped short when she came through the door, turned to everyone, and in a deep, direct voice said good morning, then walked quickly to her office. I could see her short, salt and pepper hair over the privacy wall as she made her way to her office. I let a few minutes pass, walked to the office and knocked on the door.

Staff Skipper invited me in and offered a seat. I told her how excited I was to be in S.A.C.A. I knew she had put my name forward in administrative meetings with higher ranking officers. I told her I wasn't afraid of hard work and would do my best. Staff Skipper was direct in her message and her look. She said, "That's good. I'm assigning you to Constable Darrin Kettleman. He'll be your coach officer and teach you how things work around here."

She called Kettleman and as we were waiting for him Staff Skipper told me I was being sent on the Sexual Assault and Child Abuse course at the Ontario Police College in two weeks. It was a five week course and the expectation was to pass. When Kettleman arrived, Staff Skipper handed me over. "She's all yours." Kettleman asked me to follow him and we started our day.

My first impression was he was the preppy type. He dressed well in name-brand clothes, and was probably 45. Oddly, as we walked down the hall, I noticed that for every two steps of mine, Kettleman took one. I wondered if this was a compensatory measure because he was a short man (shorter than me) compared to the average. He had big brown eyes with long eyelashes, a good-looking man.

He explained how the office functioned. There were two shifts, afternoon and day, and both were eight hours. Each officer carried a work load of between 15 and 25 cases at any given time. One of the sergeants was assigned to sift through the cases as they came in and assign them to a detective. There was always one person on call during the weekend and they were available through a beeper. Anyone arrested for sexual assault or child abuse over the weekend was the on-call person's responsibility.

Kettleman showed me how the interview rooms operated. Where we were sitting (a small area with two chairs) was where the interview was done. In the adjoining room the interview was recorded on a DVD; the assisting investigator sat in this room and took notes for future reference and court purposes. Kettleman said he would be the go-to person for any questions I might have with any of my cases. Just as we left, he cautioned me:

"Don't ever screw up. Staff Sergeant Skipper doesn't take kindly to people who screw up, and she tends to be harder on women than men for some reason."

I said it was not my intention to screw up.

Once Kettleman dealt with the preliminaries, he took me back to my office where there were already four file folders waiting. He showed me a form and told me most investigators used this form for their notes versus the traditional patrol-officer notebook. It was blank, titled 'Officer's Notes' and was used for dates, times and names of people contacted, plus their conversations. Our workstations were joined by cupboards above. I got started on my files and by the end of the day had seven open cases.

Two weeks flew by. I was adjusting to my new work environment but then the time came to go back to Ontario Police College, the place I really despised. I hadn't been there in over 15 years and wondered if it had changed at all or was the same miserable place. I left Murray and the girls who were really quite self-sufficient now — 16 and nine.

I got there, checked in, parked and unpacked the car; I made my bed and settled in for the night. I got up early the next morning so I'd be first in the shower, and then headed for the classroom. There were 25 others there, and one (much to my surprise), from my own office — Constable Ruham Beetalkie. Beetalkie, from Guyana, was a handsome guy, gentle, bright smile, white teeth; we sat in the same group.

The teacher introduced herself. She was a Deputy Chief from Vancouver and had been seconded to the OPC for the past couple of years. She was pretty, dark brown short hair, tall frame, soft smile, lots of confidence and a distinct presence. After she introduced herself, she asked us to do the same. She reviewed the course outline and explained the expectations. As she went through the outline I saw a few that intrigued me, and suddenly became eager to begin. The time there was interspersed with guest speakers as well as daily classroom lectures. We learned sections of the Criminal Code pertaining to different sexual assault offences, we became familiar with the various institutions involved in child abuse cases, we heard stories from victims who had been sexually assaulted, read profiles, and studied patterns of people who commit crimes involving sexual assaults, as well as other topics. Suddenly there was only a week to go. For four weeks I hadn't been home and was anxious for that last week to be over.

On the last day of class, after the final exam, everyone was free to go. As each member said goodbye, I reflected that the classes had been excellent and my classmates from police services throughout Ontario had brought with them many years of experience. I found the college manageable this time. It hadn't changed much, but at least I hadn't felt like a prisoner while there. This time, for the first time, I felt treated as an adult. There were no extracurricular activities to attend, I didn't have to shine my boots every night, and I got to wear my own clothes instead of a uniform. Overall, it was pretty positive. But I was glad to be back home with my family and back to work Monday morning.

I went straight to work the next day. I had a lot of catching up to do — emails, phone calls, new case files. Within a couple of weeks I was carrying a case load of about 20 files.

Having been away at OPC and now back working more closely with Kettleman, I noticed he was a glory seeker. A glory-seeker is one who gives no one else credit, seeking it all for themselves. It becomes all about them and what they did. If we worked on an involved case together, and it had a positive outcome, he took the credit because he was the lead investigator. There was never any mention of help from me or others. There were a lot of glory-seekers in the police service. I'd seen many over the years and found they each had two specific characteristics — ego and selfishness.

Glory seeking went against my grain. I was more of a team player; if the team did well, I did well.

Eight months in and I was working hard. I'd been on call over the weekend a few times and was getting a good feel for things in the office. Kettleman and I were working afternoons when a call came in with information that a young woman had been beaten and sexually assaulted at a halfway house in the west end of the City. Kettleman hung up, grabbed his notepad and coat, and beckoned to me. He explained along the way what had taken place.

By the time we arrived the female victim had been taken to the hospital by the first responding officers who brought her to the Police Station afterwards. The officer at the scene walked us through what had happened. He said the young woman working at the halfway house was approached from behind and hit over the head with a vase. She fell at the top of the staircase, the suspect grabbed her, wrapped a telephone cord around her neck and choked her.

He kicked her down the stairs, dragged her into the office, grabbed scissors from the desk, cut her clothing down the front, then down the back and sexually assaulted her. Once he'd finished, he stole some taxi chits and petty cash and left on his bicycle. The woman waited until she was sure he was gone, pulled a shower curtain from the bathroom, wrapped herself in it and ran into the street. She flagged down the first car.

After gathering as much information as they could, it then became our number one priority to find the suspect. We asked if he had relatives in the City. The on-scene officer told us the suspect had a mother in town but he hadn't seen her for many years. He could have gone to friends' houses, another halfway house, the mall, the park or the skateboard park. We gathered as much evidence as we could and asked Forensics to do the same. Witness statements had been taken by the first responding officers and turned over to us. Kettleman took the lead, as usual, and at no point did he offer me the opportunity. This was another glory-seeking opportunity.

Once back at the police station, a message was broadcast to all patrol officers with a description of the suspect and places that he frequented. Patrol units went to his friends' residences, the mall, and the parks but not his mother's residence. I asked why not; it was my opinion the mother's residence should be checked because if someone had committed a terrible crime I believed he would go and see someone he knew. In this case, as the suspect was under 18, I thought the closest person to him would be a parent. Kettleman never made the request and the mother's residence was not checked. A media bulletin was prepared and released in time for the late local news. Shortly after it was broadcast, we were told the victim and two of her friends were in the interview room. The officers discussed the case further with the investigators and were asked for copies of their notes for the file before leaving.

We gathered a few articles we needed for the interview. We introduced ourselves to the victim, Kelsey Brown, and her two friends. The three girls had agreed that once the interview started, the two friends would go home. It was obvious Kelsey was upset; she'd been crying, her eyes were puffy, cheeks flushed, and she was holding a crumpled Kleenex in her hand. I noticed she was wearing a beige, flowing, tattered top and thought to myself "It's probably one of her favourites." Kelsey's jeans were torn at the knee, the latest rage in young peoples' fashion. Kettleman told Kelsey how sorry we were this had happened. He said patrol officers were looking for the suspect and if she could offer any clues as to where he might have gone, it would be appreciated. He explained he would do the interview and I would be in the room next door taking notes and recording. Kelsey was fine with this so I went to the other room. I slipped in a tape and started to record.

As Kettleman became more acquainted with Kelsey, I noticed how well-spoken and what a strong young woman she was. At difficult moments in remembering the assault, she fought back tears, struggled through it and recalled specific details. The more she spoke the more I realized what an incredible witness she was. She became a very believable person to me. I thought, "You've just been through this horrible event, and the bravery and calmness of getting through this interview is amazing." Having worked with young offenders at the halfway house, Kelsey knew the law and how it applied to them. She was not a typical victim. She was determined and confident and communicated with Kettleman in a way I'd never seen with other victims. There were even times when her sense of humour surfaced as she tried to explain something. The interview lasted about 60 minutes and by then it was 0315 hours. I went back into the interview room as Kettleman finished the interview. Kelsey asked what would happen once the suspect was apprehended. We told her he would be taken before a judge who would request that he be held in custody because of the violence of the crime.

Kettleman asked me to make arrangements to have Kelsey picked up at the station and driven home. Kelsey told us that her friends would be waiting for her so she wouldn't be going back to an empty house. We escorted her to the lobby where a patrol officer was waiting, said goodbye and that we'd be in touch. Returning to our office, we chatted about what an incredible witness Kelsey was, and then called it a night.

The next day we were working afternoons again and we both went in a bit early to get caught up. Shortly after I got there, I got a call saying the suspect had been picked up by patrol, and officers were on the way to the station with him. I suspected we were in for another long shift.

Within the hour, the arresting officer, a Patrol Sergeant, burst into the office. "Where are the detectives investigating the Brown case," he roared. We were pointed out. He stomped towards us. The suspect had been picked up at his mother's residence, he yelled. She'd called to turn him in.

I couldn't believe my ears. The one place I thought he'd go and that's where he was apprehended!

This didn't go down well with Kettleman. He just as vehemently gave his side of the story to the Sergeant, and very quickly after the Sergeant left he said I could take lead investigator in the case. I figured he sensed something was going wrong and he didn't want his name attached; he quite blatantly was making me the scapegoat.

But, at this point, I didn't care. I grabbed the chance with both hands. This was the biggest case I'd been involved in to date and there was no way I was giving it up. There was still a lot left to do and when it came time to go to court not only would it be fascinating, it would be mine. As it turned out, the Patrol Sergeant was just blowing off steam. He never complained, there were no repercussions. I, on the other hand, got the benefit of his venting. I continued to prepare the court brief for the bail hearing the following day. It was my goal to make sure the accused was held in custody. And sure enough, the ruling was for the accused to be held in custody with a court date set for a couple of months down the road. I called Kelsey with the news; she was pleased.

Almost a year passed before the case was scheduled for court. I met with the Crown attorney and Kelsey two weeks before the court date. The Crown attorney told Kelsey there were two options. The first was to be tried as an adult; if that happened, and he was convicted, he wouldn't get an opportunity for good rehabilitation. The second was to be tried as a young person; if he was tried and convicted here he would have a lot better chance of rehabilitation — good programs and therapy. Kelsey chose option two. I was amazed again at Kelsey's maturity, strength and courage; she was looking ahead as to what was best for the accused, not acting in revenge.

Two weeks later the accused was found guilty. He was sentenced to the maximum in young offenders court — five years in jail with no chance of parole. Kelsey was happy but now it was time for us to say goodbye. This was difficult because we'd developed a strong bond, both working and friendship. Outside the courthouse we hugged and I wished Kelsey all the best in life. Kelsey thanked me for all the hard work and a good final outcome. And then she said, "I'm glad you were the investigator in the end. I really didn't like that other guy." She said I'd shown compassion and strength while leading her through the legal side of things, and it was me who helped give her the courage to endure the journey. I wiped away my tears and said a final goodbye.

Driving home after work, looking forward to the weekend, I reflected how police work with all its ups and downs can still be rewarding. It doesn't have to be the people you work with that make it that way but the people you serve. It made some of the hard times worthwhile and satisfying. After a good couple of days off with Murray and the kids, I felt pretty good. I was happy with the outcome of the case and grateful for my family.

A new week began and the files continued to pour in. I received one file that was a bit quirky and had to consult with Kettleman. We discussed it in detail and had decided what to do when Staff Sergeant Skipper approached us. Kettleman briefed her and after further discussion it was decided the file should be sent to courts to have a Crown attorney review it. I sent the entire file to courts that day requesting a review and to get it back to me within two weeks, before my holidays began. As long as the file was back within that time I'd have time to complete it according to the Crown's specifications, after review. The accused's first court appearance was scheduled while I was on holidays and this is why I wanted to deal with it before leaving.

In this particular case, the accused had been released on a Notice to Appear. When an officer issues a Notice to Appear, they not only include a court date on the document but also a fingerprint date. If the accused fails to show for either of these dates, he/she can be re-arrested for fail to appear. The way the process works is the Notice to Appear is forwarded to the court clerk's office with the file and they are filed according to court date. If the accused does not appear in court or for fingerprints on the set date, an arrest warrant is issued. In this case, the Notice to Appear was filed under the court date but the rest of the file was forwarded to the Crown's office; they had been separated. A week passed and I'd still not heard back from courts. I called the court office and asked if they could track the file. They found it and told me it was sitting on the Crown's desk for review. I waited until the second last day

A New Experience

before the beginning of my holidays; still no reply from the Crown. I sent courts an email requesting the file be returned and again received no response.

A week and a half into my vacation, I received a call at home. Most of the time we took vacations out of the country so we wouldn't be bothered by work, but this time we'd remained at home. I answered the call and Kettleman was on the other end.

"Staff Skipper wants you back in the office immediately," he said.

She wanted me to deal with the file that had been left on the Crown attorney's desk. One of the court clerks had found the Notice to Appear and when the accused showed up in court there was no paperwork to go along with it; they couldn't find the file.

I dropped everything and headed to the office. When I arrived, Staff Sergeant Skipper asked what had happened with the file. I explained I'd done everything I could prior to leaving on holidays; I showed her my email proof of work. This wasn't enough for her. She demanded I go to the court house and straighten the issue out.

Off I went, and then to the Crown attorney's office. I sat down with the Crown to review the file and then sent it to the court office. All was in order. I went back and told Staff Skipper it was done.

"Don't let that happen again," she snapped.

Needless to say the rest of my holiday was ruined. I felt uneasy and anxious.

I returned to work not knowing what was in store, but was ready for anything. During my shift, Staff Sergeant Skipper told me that the Sergeant who assigns files was going on holidays and I was to replace him. I said sure, anything to help the office. This was going to happen next week and this week I could sit with him and learn the ropes. While the other Sergeant was on holidays I was assigned to the position permanently. This meant that the majority of my time was spent assigning files, not investigating them.

I started to notice little things that Staff Skipper did to make me feel uncomfortable. She was friendlier with the other staff members. She pushed me hard with my work and then expected more. She told me I would have to carry my own work load in addition to hers when she was away on holidays. One day I was in the office with three other staff members and Staff Skipper started to question me about the Staff Sergeant's job. I knew nothing about the job as I'd never filled in for a Staff Sergeant before. Staff Skipper made me look and feel incompetent in front of the others because I didn't have all the answers. It got to the point where one of the other staff members passed by my desk, behind Staff Sergeant Skipper, looked at me, and rolled her eyes as if to say, "Are you kidding me?" I was sure the other staff member was being supportive but when Staff Skipper finished, I left the office as quickly as I could. I was humiliated, frustrated and longed for a time when I wouldn't have to deal with bullies. I had no more energy and felt broken. I cried.

As each day passed, my anxiety grew. I no longer felt wanted or part of the team. It was so bad that I asked to leave. I went to Staff Skipper, told her what I wanted and Staff Skipper simply asked, "Where do you want to go?" I didn't know; I just wanted out from underneath Staff Skipper's command. I said, "Send me to the road. I've worked there forever, so just send me to the road." Within one week that's where I found myself.

It was my last day in S.A.C.A. Staff Skipper told everyone we were scheduled to have a picture taken in the lobby at 1100 hours with a section meeting afterwards in the boardroom. I

A New Experience

told her I had no intention of having my picture taken with the section. I didn't feel part of the team and wouldn't be in the picture. When 1100 hours rolled around and the rest of the staff went to the lobby, I went down the hallway towards the board room. While heading down the hall I ran into my Inspector and stopped to have a chat with him. He was not just my boss but also Staff Skipper's. As we stood in the hallway talking, Staff Skipper suddenly came around the corner like a bull with smoke coming out her nose. She stomped up to me and said between gritted teeth "Get down to that lobby now!" Her face was red. Staff Skipper, it was obvious, hated anyone who said "No" to her. I looked at the Inspector. "I better be going," I said. As I walked downstairs to the lobby I started crying. I stood in the lobby along with the rest of them, red eyes and all. I headed to the boardroom afterwards and sat quietly at the table throughout the section meeting. Then I headed back to my office and packed my things. I said goodbye to those who were there and headed to my locker.

I tried to figure out what had gone wrong. Was it the file I had to fix over the holidays, or did Staff Skipper just decide she didn't like me once I was in her section. No one ever told me I was doing a poor job. It became simply an unsolved mystery to me. It should be noted that Staff Sergeant Skipper when interviewed by CBC news upon her retirement was quoted saying "I think we should be role-modelling just being nice and being kind." She added "that it is her hope that caring for people will be both her legacy and the forces motto moving forward."

—14—

Gearing Down and Looking Toward Retirement

I was back on F Platoon and in the south end of the city. This was definitely my comfort zone. I knew the road like the back of my hand. It was the spring of 2009.

Now that I was back, I had a plan leading to retirement. I wanted to be transferred from the road to the Information Desk as soon as possible. If I could manage that, it would take me through to my retirement date — January 31, 2011. I wanted the transfer because it would mean fewer arrests which translated into fewer court appearances in my retirement, and there were no night shifts. I didn't tell anyone my plans because I was superstitious enough to believe the minute I told someone it wouldn't happen. People would go out of their way to make it not happen. Somehow, within six months, I got my transfer.

The Information Desk, generally speaking, is where constables are sent if they are pregnant, injured, or if they get themselves into trouble. Their job is to greet the public and take any relevant reports. The number of officers working at the Information Desk varies. There are two Sergeants assigned and a Staff Sergeant who oversees the section. The

Sergeant's job is to supervise the officers along with other administrative duties.

The layout and location of the Information Desk is designed to be part of the lobby. That means when members of the public enter, the Information Desk is obvious and visible. The desk that the officers sit at is elevated so we can speak with the public at eye level and it is enclosed by bullet-proof glass. There are seven work stations, two for civilian members and five for officers. The Sergeants sat in a back office connected to the same area the officers worked in. There were two desks facing one another and two filing cabinets.

I took over a retiring Sergeant's position. The second Sergeant was leaving in two weeks; he had opted to quit the Police Service. I spent two weeks training and learned quickly that one of my major roles was scheduling. As each new officer arrived at the desk they would be incorporated into the schedule. Some officers had to be gradually re-introduced into the work place and could only work two days a week; others worked full time, all the time. The schedule could change six or more times a day so both officers and Sergeants had to be on top of who was working when and ensure there was proper coverage.

The end of the two weeks came and I was going solo until a second Sergeant was found to replace the one who quit. I learned the job quickly and was efficient at it. Within no time at all things were running smoothly and a second Sergeant was found. His name was Veto Mirelli. Mirelli landed at the Information Desk because he had just been diagnosed with multiple sclerosis and couldn't work patrol. He was a short, Italian man who told me he liked to spend a lot of money on hair products. His full, dark, head of hair complimented his fair skin and his warm smile. He wore dark-framed glasses that reminded me of the Mrs. Beasly doll from a TV show I used to watch as a kid. He liked to let his beard grow a couple of days because he felt this made him look more attractive.

I had never met or worked with Mirelli, and was hoping things would work out well. After we got to know one another, we got along great. We worked our shifts to cover off the utmost time during peak hours. One of us worked days, the other afternoons, and if special circumstances arose, we worked things out between us. There was only one officer on the desk overnight; he worked alone and required very little supervision.

When Mirelli first came to the desk I trained him on everything I'd learned. Over time, however, he decided he didn't like the scheduling part of things and let me handle it. I didn't mind at first but as time went on I found other things he wouldn't do, and I had to pick up the slack. When I asked him about it he laughed and said he forgot, or didn't like doing that particular job. Eventually I was doing the majority of the work and Mirelli was just coming to work where he sat at his desk and talked to me. I was frustrated and told him. He picked up the slack for a couple of days and then slipped back again until, one day, he got the surprise of his life. He was told he would be supervising an officer who was being transferred to the desk the following Monday. He would have to make weekly reports on his progress.

Both of us knew of this officer and that he was a challenge-and-a-half. He had been passed from section to section because no one knew how to handle him, or what to do with him. He had some personal health issues that prevented him from being on patrol but even during the time he had been on patrol he received complaints from both officers and the public. This officer was a walking time bomb with a temper to boot. He said whatever he wanted, whenever he wanted, appropriate or not. He lacked filters that most of us have. He was tall and handsome, and kept his body in the shape of a professional body builder. His smile would charm anyone. Unfortunately for him he also suffered from fainting episodes. This kept him from driving a car and so he had to take the bus to and from work. His name was Constable Martin Everet.

It was Friday when we learned about Everet coming to the Information Desk and we were both taken aback. But the fact that Mirelli had been put in charge of his supervision pleased me, as my plate was already full. The weekly reports and close supervision that Everet required actually balanced responsibilities somewhat between the two of us. We discussed Everet and Mirelli said he would come up with a plan over the weekend to supervise him properly.

Monday arrived and so did Everet. We welcomed him to the Information Desk. Mirelli took him to a back office to discuss his plans and the expectations he had of Everet while working at the Information Desk.

Weeks passed and Everet was adjusting well. He needed reminders every so often but, all in all, was doing well. I was going on vacation in a couple of weeks and had to review the administrative duties, once again, with Mirelli. When I got back I heard that things had not gone well.

According to Mirelli, about four days after I left, Everet passed out in the office.

"I was sitting right here talking to him. He was in your chair. I looked in his direction and his eyes were glazed over. I called out to him and next thing he was on the floor. When he came to, he was combative and it took four of us to get him onto the paramedic stretcher.

"After that incident he returned to work a couple of days later, and didn't he pass out a second time! I had to grab him from behind to keep him from falling and he hasn't been back to work since."

Gearing Down and Looking Toward Retirement

I was amazed at what Mirelli told me. As a precaution, I discussed safety with him; if it took four officers to put Everet on the gurney, that could jeopardize all officers and sergeants down the road. Mirelli said we would continue to work with Everet as he worked through things with his doctor.

Several months passed and Everet was given the green light to return to work. He was on medication and as his passing-out episodes had subsided, his doctor felt that it was safe for him to return. I was six months away from retirement and wanted nothing more than a quiet exit. I watched as Mirelli worked with Everet daily and admired him for the way he handled him. I could tell there was a mutual respect between the two.

Life carried on at the Information Desk, officers came and went, other officers had babies and Everet was transferred from the desk to Human Resources. Mirelli was still responsible for his weekly reports but it was decided that his skills would best be utilized in Human Resources.

I was on the countdown; I could hardly wait for my last day of work. I didn't want any parties but told the Old Gloucester Girls if they wanted to do something small I'd appreciate that more than anything. Murray also decided to retire at that time and both of us would retire on the same day. I'd be 50 and Murray 54. We had our health and were about to set sail on a new journey. We wanted to spend more time with family, do some travelling and make use of the new Seadoos we'd bought as retirement gifts. We wanted to do more boating, ATVing and simply enjoy life. We planned our own retirement party, in the comfort of our own home, with family, neighbours, and good friends. It was set for a couple of months after our final day, to celebrate 28 years of policing for me and 32 years of policing for Murray.

My last day of work arrived and the people I worked with at the Information Desk hosted a luncheon for me. They invited

Murray to share the fun. They presented me with a gift and said some kind words. A representative from the Police Association showed up and presented both of us with a spousal pin, significant because it is in recognition of the sacrifice the supporting spouse makes while a member of the police service is working. It was an enjoyable event. Everyone was socializing and eating when suddenly I saw Nic Flagherty in the room. My instinct was to go over and tell him to get out; I restrained myself. I knew I was bigger than that, and let it be. I did ask Murray, under my breath, though, "What the hell is he doing here?"

"I have no idea," he said.

My last thoughts were "They have to follow you out the door, to the bitter end. They can't leave you in peace."

I gathered my things, thanked everyone for the gift and the kind words and walked out the door with Murray by my side, my head high. I was proud of myself for what I'd endured over the past 28 years, but it was not without a cost. I hoped I'd made a difference in society, and for the women of tomorrow, both reasons I'd joined the police service for in the first place.

Chief Vern White presenting me with my retirement badge

www.ingramcontent.com/pod-product-compliance
Lightning Source LLC
Chambersburg PA
CBHW070917080526
44589CB00013B/1328